THE WOMAN'S CLUB OF EVANSTON

A HISTORY

T0308795

The
Woman's Club
of Evanston
A History

Written and researched by
Erin Hvizdak

Epilogue by
Kathy Rocklin

With additional material by
Vickie Burke,
Jan Hartwell,
and **Alicia O'Connor**

The Woman's Club of Evanston
Evanston, Illinois

The Woman's Club of Evanston
1702 Chicago Avenue
Evanston, Illinois 60201

www.wcofe.org

First edition. First printing.
ISBN 978-0-578-49487-6

Photos courtesy of Evanston Photographic Studio, Robert Shiverts Photography, Jennifer Schuman, Woman's Club of Evanston Archives, and Woman's Club of Evanston Capital Campaign, unless otherwise credited.

Book designed and typeset by Marianne Jankowski

Additional copies of this book may be ordered from the Chicago Distribution Center, 1-800-621-2736, or online at www.nupress.northwestern.edu.

Printed in the United States of America.

To every member of the Club—
past, present, and future

CONTENTS

World War II: Leading on the Home Front
Building Morale through the Arts
Adjusting to the Changing Needs

Why is it important to document and produce an independently researched and written book of the history of the Woman's Club of Evanston? What possible usefulness and importance did an organization made
up of only women have when it was created, and what is its significance
in this day and age? How has the Evanston community benefited, grown,
and prospered because of the work of the Woman's Club?

These questions are frequently asked as a challenge to why the Woman's
Club of Evanston has been, and still is in today's world, a relevant organization. All these questions are answered in this deliberate and extraordinary document of the history of the Woman's Club, and by default a
history of Evanston, our nation, and world events.

The creation, growth, and continued work of the Woman's Club of
Evanston has been a direct reaction to address community needs and
especially the needs of the most vulnerable in our community. Its activities range from toy drives for needy children to supporting organizations
dealing with housing and health issues specifically related to women and
children, quality education opportunities, and veteran support. Such
needs never seem to go away, but they manifest themselves in different
ways, and the Woman's Club of Evanston has always strived to maintain a
flexible attitude and to react appropriately at different times in our history.

The 125th Anniversary Committee commissioned this book. Many of
us have heard the Club stories and folklore shared among the membership informally over the years, and we have amassed a large archive of
material—scrapbooks, Club publications, articles, and records—that is
of historical interest. We decided that in honor of our 125th anniversary
year we owed it to ourselves, and to every member who came before us
and those who will come after, to create a proper, thoroughly researched
document of our history. Those of us who have seen this project through
to completion had little idea at the start of the incredible significance of
what we would find.

I hope you read this book with an open mind to the issues and outside influences that existed in our community, the nation, and the world over the decades. The Woman's Club of Evanston was organized at a time when women had no rights and were basically considered property owned and managed by a husband, father, or brother. Women could not vote or own real estate and had very limited access to education. Yet they organized, gained influence, and began to change the world around them. The Woman's Club of Evanston grew and changed with the times, making a concerted effort to constantly reevaluate, adapt, and evolve.

The Woman's Club of Evanston—empowering women for 130 years and counting.

Vickie Burke
President, 2000–2001
January 2019

ACKNOWLEDGMENTS

Vickie Burke for her leadership, input, financial support, and devotion from the initial concept through completion.

Kathy Rocklin, President during our 125th Celebration year, for her unwavering commitment to and extraordinary work toward the completion of this book.

History Book Completion Committee 2016–2019:
Natalie Banovitz, Vickie Burke, Lori Osborne, and Kathy Rocklin

History Book Initial Committee 2011–2014: Jane DeMoss, Chair, Erin Hvizdak, Researcher, Natalie Banovitz, Debbie Cassell, Terry Dason, Carla Ford, Kris Hartzell, and Lori Osborne

125th Anniversary Committee: Vickie Burke, Chair
Fern Allison, Natalie Banovitz, Sara Brenner, Donna Brown, Julie Chernoff, Mary Kay Conlon, Terry Dason, Jane DeMoss, Sara Dioguardi, Donna Frett, Beth Geiger, Anne Gilford, Kris Hartzell, Jan Hazlett, Wendy Irwin, Angelique Ketzback, Sally Mabadi, Tammy McKnight, Loreen Mershimer, Lori Osborne, Anita Remijas, Kathy Rocklin, and Trimmy Stamell

Financial support:
Fern Allison, Diane Bailey, Anne Berkeley, Jackie Brennan, Sara Brenner, Cynthia Bridges, Gabrielle Brooks, Donna Brown, Ginny Buerger, Vickie Burke, Emily Caragher, Amy Ceisel, Julie Chernoff, Barb Cochran, Kate Collinson, Martha Conley, Paula Danoff, Terry Dason, Fran Dietzgen, Sara Dioguardi, Melody Farley, Donna Frett, Beth Geiger, Anne Gilford, Diane Golan, Jenni Gordon, Betsy Graham, Susan Hammer, Lisa Hurst Hatton, Beverly Heimann, Marilyn Hendershot, Muffy Hendershot, Pam Hess, Laurie Howick, Susan Jeffers, Angelique Ketzback, Marjorie Leventhal, Jane Liechty,

Kate Mahoney, Kate Mattson, Tamara McKnight, Loreen Mershimer, Lisa Miceli, Edith Molumby, Lori Osborne, Anita Remijas, Barbara Rittenhouse, Kathy Rocklin, Mimi Roeder, Heather Silver, Linda Sienkiewicz, Kate Spector, Patty Sprague, Trimble Stamell, Natalie Tate, Linda Walker, Frieda Walter, Bonnie Wefler, Elizabeth Weislogel, and Chava Wu

Additional thanks to Janet Olson from Northwestern University Deering Library for her invaluable help with the Woman's Club Archives, Lauri Whiskeyman for her editing and proofreading skills, Siobhan Drummond for editorial and production support, and Marianne Jankowski for graphic design.

CHARTER MEMBERS

In memoriam
Elizabeth Boynton Harbert, PhD
Founder and First President, 1889–1897

Miss Mary M. Baker

Mrs. Charles H. Betts

Mrs. Elizabeth S. Bliss

Mrs. John E. Blunt

Mrs. Henry L. Boltwood

Mrs. E. R. Chapman

Mrs. Winchester E. Clifford

Mrs. N. Arthur Coble

Mrs. Henry B. Craigin

Mrs. Edwin A. Dawson

Miss Sarah S. Dickinson

Mrs. William C. Dickinson

Mrs. Henry J. Edwards

Mrs. D. B. Foote

Mrs. O. Clinton French

Mrs. Orvis French

Mrs. H. H. Gage

Mrs. Charles F. Grey

Mrs. H. W. Hinsdale

Mrs. H. H. Kingsley

Mrs. E. W. Learned

Mrs. P. L. McKinnie

Mrs. R. B. McMullen

Mrs. J. E. Miller

Mrs. George D. Moseley

Miss Caroline A. Murray

Mrs. L. D. Norton

Mrs. H. F. Olmsted

Miss Kate C. Quinlan

Mrs. Louise Quinlan

Mrs. F. D. Raymond

Mrs. George B. Reynolds

Mrs. W. T. Rickards

Mrs. George M. Sargent

Mrs. Nels E. Simon

Mrs. Thaddeus P. Stanwood

Mrs. Herbert Streeter

Mrs. A. F. Townsend

Mrs. S. Van Benschoten

Mrs. E. M. Vandercook

Mrs. C. H. Zimmerman

Elizabeth Boynton Harbert
Founder and First President

CHAPTER ONE

Building a Foundation: 1889 to 1913

Let a club with such a membership as this of ours in Evanston, highly resolve to so concentrate and distribute its forces that its benign influence shall extend not only to every child, but to every home; not only to the children, but to all the animals and birds; not only to the animals and birds but to the trees and vines and flowers, and soon the aggregate result would create for a surprised and happy world, glimpses of a new heaven and a new earth.

—Elizabeth Boynton Harbert
Founder and President, 1889–1897

And So It Began

For women in Evanston, gathering to discuss pressing social issues was nothing new, especially when it involved Elizabeth Boynton Harbert. Harbert was born in 1843 and grew up in Crawfordsville, Indiana. She was educated at the Western College for Women in Oxford, Ohio, and at Terre Haute Female College, where she graduated with honors. She married Captain William S. Harbert in 1874, and they moved to Evanston. They had two daughters, Corinne and Boynton, and a son, Arthur, who died when he was still in his twenties.

Having served as president of the Illinois Woman Suffrage Association for twelve years, Harbert, affectionately known as "Lizzie," was no stranger to assembling both women and men to work for the betterment of social conditions. On March 2, 1889, Harbert invited "a pleasant coterie of women" to her home for a "very informal little gathering" at what is now 1412 Judson Avenue in Evanston to discuss the possibility of forming a club that would bring together "women of thought and experience . . . to compare views and if possible, devise ways and means for securing better education, better amusement, better household service, and a truer philosophy of life than that yet achieved."

Harbert wanted to put women's knowledge into practice, particularly applying it to the rapid national changes triggered by increasing urbanization and immigration. Echoing the feeling of many of the forty-two charter members, Jane Zimmerman reflected in "Reminiscences of 30 Years": "I wanted to get away from the kitchen drain and dwell, for an hour, in a higher atmosphere. I remember many of the ladies had the same feeling, that we wanted to learn something worthwhile; in the time-honored phrase — 'Improve our minds.'"

Knowing of Harbert's background in political activism, Mrs. Louise Brockaway Stanwood, first vice-president and second president of the Woman's Club of Evanston, voiced her initial concerns: "At our first meeting at Mrs. Harbert's, we were all very much afraid Mrs. Harbert would try to put something over on us about suffrage — and think of how we look at suffrage today." However, Nellie Kingsley, third president of the Club, recalled that Harbert "always withheld her own opinions unless questioned, and then stated them in so modest a fashion as greatly to impress those who heard her." But this club was not primarily about suffrage; it was about improving the lives not only of the women members but of the wider community and, by extension, the world.

Most of the early members were wives of high-ranking professionals in Evanston, including professors at Northwestern University, clergy, lawyers, businessmen, and school administrators, and they had leisure time, college degrees, and the support and connections of their spouses. Most of them already belonged to philanthropic associations and literary and social clubs. They had families and their own lines of work, their own interests. Harbert, in her resignation speech in April 1897, explained why it was so crucial to have the Woman's Club in this town, why clubs are so crucial in every town: "The greatest obstacle to overcome in our busy university town, amid the unusual environments or conditions of a rapidly growing suburb of a phenomenal city, was lack of time on the part of many representative women, already officially connected with reformatory or philanthropic work." She went on to say that a well-organized club that brings together literary, educational, artistic, ethical, social, religious, and domestic interests would "prove a great conservator of time."

Evanston had scarcely five thousand citizens when the women first assembled in 1889, but its population was booming. Northwestern University had been founded in 1851, and the Great Chicago Fire of 1871 had forced many people to migrate out of the city. Evanston was incorporated as a town in 1863 and as a city in 1892. Evanston was known as the City of Homes because it was essentially residential. It offered an escape from the poverty and crowding of Chicago, and from 1885 to 1920, new residents built homes and neighborhoods here. The Woman's Club of Evanston was formed during this time of great change and possibility. Recognizing that they could make a profound impact on bettering the conditions of the community, the members began to carve out their own space and foundation in both the Evanston scene and the national landscape.

Although opportunities for women generally were still limited at the end of the nineteenth century, many of the early members came from families of means and had been encouraged to pursue their education, holding degrees from institutions such as Wellesley, Northwestern, Vassar, and Smith. Times were indeed changing for women: the number of women enrolled in coeducational institutions of higher learning jumped from four thousand in 1872 to forty thousand by 1890, in addition to all of the women enrolled in women's colleges. Yet even with the rise of educated women, working outside of the home was not popular with everyone in this socioeconomic strata. "Not many years past were a woman asked to write on the subject of 'The Relation of the Woman's Club to the Community,' she would have been placed immediately on the defensive," Harriet Clifton, Club president from 1911 to 1913, wrote, "for Club life for women conveyed the idea of neglected homes and children; the Club was an organization detrimental to progress and humanity." President Grover Cleveland at one time stated, "Without exaggeration of statement we may assume that there are woman's clubs whose objects and intents are not only harmful, but harmful in a way that directly menaces the integrity of our homes." And yet, the women who started the Club did not let this negative sentiment stop them; they did not believe that working for the betterment of society made them any less of a wife or mother, and they refused to sit idly by with their education, experience, and economic standing. Rather, they acknowledged their privileged positions and sought to use them for good, to improve the lives of those less fortunate.

The Women's Club Movement

Friends, beloved, all hail! to these possibilities of individual and associated effort, and with renewed consecration let us grasp the bloodless, unstained, yet potent and invincible weapon—i.e., a Woman's Club.

—Elizabeth Boynton Harbert
Founder and President, 1889–1897

The women's club movement was quickly taking shape all across the country. On March 20, 1889, the same month and year that the Woman's Club of Evanston first assembled, ninety-seven existing women's clubs from around the country gathered in New York to discuss how these organizations could collaborate for the betterment of both themselves and society. From this meeting, the General Federation of Women's Clubs (GFWC) was created, adopting as their motto, "We look for unity, but unity in diversity."

Women's clubs had already existed for decades, addressing such areas as moral reform and the education of women. During the Civil War, women's charitable organizations formed and grew in numbers, providing needed services to populations such as wounded soldiers and orphans of war. The founders of the modern-day women's club are considered to be Sorosis (New York City) and the New England Women's Club (Boston), both created in 1868. These years of activity and leadership gave women the courage and inspiration to draw on their strengths to better the world for their families and others in need. At the same time, opportunities for women were increasing and the birth rate was falling, while new technologies of transportation and communication were allowing a particular coterie of educated, confident, and worldly women to assemble and communicate more easily.

But with these changing conditions came increased urbanization and thus a host of other concerns related to health, education, crime, and the economy. Lacking the vote, and seeing that societal needs were not being addressed, groups such as the Woman's Club of Evanston sought to use their economic and social standing, and common positions as women and mothers, to establish solidarity and help those most vulnerable to worsening urban conditions. If the order of society and the home were to be protected from crime, disease, and general moral and physical decay, many women felt that it was their "higher calling" to attack the root of the problem. Specifically, club women wanted to prove themselves as "better ladies rather than deserters of the home" by pursuing reforms that fit into this ideal of womanhood and motherhood so that no one could question their motives. Harbert saw this potential to enact change in many of the women she had met in Evanston.

Our First Year

The first official meeting of the Woman's Club of Evanston was on March 23, 1889, and featured a reading of national women's rights activist Julia Ward Howe's 1873 essay "How Can Women Best Associate?" An inspiration to women's groups for decades, it focused on the need for a woman's club in every region, emphasized that women should be self-sacrificing for the good of the community, and provided practical advice about the governance of clubs. Women's associations were not to assemble for solely social purposes or without direction, rather, "an Association of Women should not exist long without asking itself: 'What are the most pressing needs of society, and what can we, as a body corporate, do to meet and answer them?'" Furthermore, Howe wrote, "deliberation in common, mutual instruction, achievement for the whole, better and more valuable than the individual success of any, these should be the objects had and held constantly in view. . . . Our motto must be, The good of all the aim of each."

The road map for women's organizations was still being created in 1889, so each club had to organize based on the needs of its local community and its members. In its first year, the Woman's Club of Evanston undertook courses of study to pursue "mutual self-improvement." For example, the second meeting required members to contribute items about the women of the Revolution, or patriotic selections in honor of the centennial celebration. Presentations were diverse and included biographical studies on such women as Abigail Adams, Mary Ball Washington, Helen Hunt

Location of the first gathering of the Woman's Club of Evanston, 1889.

Jackson, and Marion Harland (the pen name of Mary Virginia Terhune). Harbert explained in her resignation speech that they studied these biographies so that members might become more aware of the possibilities that exist in every individual. These studies were meant to prepare women to participate in any social or professional circle or situation in which they found themselves. These were not fleeting exercises but a means to give women increased mobility, to increase their self-esteem, to inspire them, and to set the stage for the decades of work the Club was about to undertake.

Under Harbert's direction, the women immediately set themselves on a course of community service that remains the mission of the Club today. Clifton reiterated this aspect of the Club's mission: "Women of today recognize that their duties lie not alone in the home, but in society at large — in doing the greatest good to the greatest number possible."

In 1889, one of the first acts of charity was to provide toys to each child in need in Evanston. "Mrs. Harbert proposed that every poor little girl in town should have a doll. . . . Mrs. McKinnie tells me there were four hundred," recalled Zimmerman. "They were loaded into clothes baskets and sons of members who had horses and carriages carried them around to the poor people." The boys were not forgotten, as told by Alice Moseley in "Reminiscences":

> One thing showed Mrs. Harbert knew something about boys. Somebody suggested that the boys should have something that would be harmless, but she said, "No, every boy is going to have a knife, and a good knife, too!" and she went quietly and bought them, so that the boys should be sure to have knives.

The next year, on December 24, 1890, the Club handed out toys to an estimated two hundred children, whose "merry voices and happy faces made a bright picture of holiday cheer."

Formalizing the Organization

The Woman's Club of Evanston adopted its constitution on March 29, 1890, one year after the women first assembled in Harbert's home. Stanwood, in the Club's first five-year history, noted, "Early in the season of 1890, such a marked growth in membership and interest was perceptible, that a constitution was adopted and regular officers elected." The Evanston Press reported that the Club had almost reached its cap of seventy-five members by the second meeting, and each member was charged annual dues of 25 cents. The Club adopted as its motto, "In essentials, unity; in non-essentials, liberty; in all things, charity," a phrase attributed to a Lutheran pastor from the seventeenth century and used by numerous Protestant-based organizations in the centuries following. The Club's objects, as given in the constitution, were "mutual helpfulness in all affairs of life, and united efforts toward the higher development of humanity." Loosely following the advice Howe laid out in her essay, the organization created the roles of president, four vice presidents, a recording secretary, a corresponding secretary, a treasurer, a board of nine directors, and chairs of departments, which shifted throughout the years as the needs of the

Original Club crest

Club changed. Women were elected to their positions, and all Club matters were to be passed by a majority vote. Among these early officers was Frances Willard, second president of the Woman's Christian Temperance Union, who served as the fourth vice president during the 1891–92 Club year. The Club bylaws could be changed upon vote of the board. This parliamentary procedure ensured that all voices would be heard.

In May 1897, a new parliamentary drill was introduced to allow members to present information, ideas, or actions to the group, which could be passed, carried, tabled, denied, or otherwise dealt with. This was a style of governance pursued by woman's clubs all over the nation and meant to ensure efficiency, order, and fairness in club business. Elections for board positions, the division of the club into departments and committees, and decisions to send delegates to other organizations in the region and nationally all followed this type of procedure, as did the way meetings were run, with their established order of approving previous minutes, presenting the program or business, and allowing for discussion as necessary. Following these steps allowed the women to hone their public speaking and decision-making skills, which they hoped would transfer into larger organizations and even government. In order to practice parliamentary procedure, the women also studied it throughout the early decades of the Club, which strengthened their efforts to support or block proposed legislation. They could not yet vote, but they knew that they could still make their voices heard, so they looked for these loopholes of participation.

Serving as an officer was not an easy task, and many of the women did not quite know what they were in for. Martha White Hildreth, corresponding secretary during the 1896–97 Club year and president from 1915 to 1917, recalled:

> During the afternoon they had an election, and someone
> rose and suggested that I should run for the office of
> corresponding secretary. . . . I was so terrified and so
> embarrassed that I didn't know enough to get up and say
> I wouldn't do it, and so I promptly found myself elected.
> I asked the woman why she did such a thing, and she said
> she had told them "Don't let her know anything about it,
> because if you do, she won't take the office."

On becoming president after Harbert's tenure, Stanwood expressed that "it certainly was a case of 'fools step in where angels fear to tread' because who was I to stand in Mrs. Harbert's shoes?" The annual report of 1897 indicated that at one time "members were begged to sacrifice themselves upon the altars of office," but now "election to these offices is recognized as an expression of the highest honor of appreciation. Such has been the

growth of eight years." As the Club grew in size and status in these years, it became a privilege to be a member and leader of the organization.

The cap on membership was raised to 150 members in 1891 and then to 300 in 1896. Demand was so high that membership cards were printed and a doorman was paid $1.00 per meeting to verify the women's membership status. Emma Webster, President from 1904 to 1906, explained that in the early days "it was a very easy matter at that time to join the Club. Somebody proposed the name, and they voted on you, and if you were not blackballed, you were announced next meeting as a member." Very early on, a Reception Committee was formed to introduce new members to the group and acclimate them to the Club. This committee, which later became the Hospitality Committee and then was absorbed into the Membership Committee, continues to play an integral part in the life of the Club, helping to ensure a steady stream of members joining, remaining, and contributing.

As the Club grew larger, having a specific role gave each woman a sense of purpose. Rules, officers, and official meeting minutes held the group accountable for their actions and proved to the doubting public that time spent away from their "womanly" duties as wives and mothers was valuable and necessary. Running the Club like a business and under parliamentary procedure gave them legitimacy and put them on par with men's organizations. This may have also quelled some of the early members' hesitations; as Harbert explained in her resignation speech, "at first there was some opposition, some timidity, because of the absence of rigid rules and an iron-clad constitution." In March 1891, Moseley wrote in the annual report that, even in this university town, "it is a surprise to many that the plans for the Woman's Club have been so successfully carried out." The Club signaled that they were a strong, permanent public force to effect positive change in their community.

The members recognized that much could be accomplished when they gathered together. The women valued not only the number of members but also their diverse viewpoints and experiences. The first annual report (1891) states:

> With very few exceptions the members of the Club are
> mothers. . . . we wish to impart these women with their
> varied interests and experience and the meeting together

of those whose different training has created such varied results [that] might be helpful in giving their characters a beauty and truth, a something more complete that could only be conceived under the different lights."

The convergence of these many different viewpoints and strengths has continued to sustain the Club in its service and philanthropic efforts.

Meetings and Departments of Work

The Club began to take out advertisements for meetings and programs in Evanston newspapers when mailing the meeting announcements became too expensive. Kingsley, in "Reminiscences," expressed some of the challenges in the early years:

> I rather appreciated the difficulties, because in those days there were no telephones, no automobiles, and I used to tramp from one end of the town to the other because I was corresponding secretary. It seems to me that I did nothing else that year but address postal cards because in those days we didn't have the money that we have now, and the cards all had to be written, and it was some job to write out two or three hundred. The work seemed stupendous.

The Club established four committees in the first years: Philanthropy and Reform, Literature, World's Fair, and Social Science, which were converted to the Departments of Philanthropy and Sociology, Child and Home, and Fine Arts by 1894–95. Throughout the Club's history, all three of these departments continued under different names, and numerous committees were formed as the need arose, as detailed in the Club's yearbooks and calendars.

The departments took turns presenting programs at the general monthly all-Club meetings. Starting in 1897, each department received $25 to use in preparing its program, an amount that increased to $100 by May 1911. This format allowed the women to discover connections among their separate pursuits, provided cohesiveness to the Club, and encouraged partnerships and collaboration among members. These presentations also

SUBJECTS OF MEETINGS.

1889-1890.

March   2.   First Meeting. Organization.
March   23.   How Can Women Best Associate? Paper
              prepared by Julia W. Howe.
April   26.   Women of the Revolution.
Oct.   26.   Purpose and Origin of Woman's Clubs.
              Papers prepared by Julia W. Howe and
              Miss Edith Thomas.
Nov.   23.   Reception to the Lady Teachers of Evans-
              ton.   Address by Colonel F. Parker,
              Englewood.
Jan.   25.   Travels in Russia and Finland.   Dr. Alice B.
              Stockham.
Feb.   15.   Discussion of Constitution.
March   8.   The Place of Music in the Education of a
              Child. Miss Maria Hofer, Chicago.

NOTE—During the first year of the Club the meetings were held
every three weeks and were very informal. The members presided
in turn, and no permanent records were kept.

provided women opportunities to sharpen their leadership, research, and public speaking skills, essential abilities when venturing out of the home to enact change in the community.

The first years of programs at general Club meetings were based largely on discussions of existing literature or information from experts in various fields. During 1894–95, the Club introduced a lecture and discussion format that focused on presentations by members. Through these first years and beyond, the women used their connections to bring in prominent speakers who were experts in their respective fields. The 1894–95 year alone was packed with famous social activists, including Jane Addams, founder of Chicago's Hull House; Florence Kelley, cofounder of the NAACP, a labor activist, and chief factory inspector for the state of Illinois in 1893; and Emily Huntington Miller, a well-known children's author, educator, temperance reformer, and dean of women at Northwestern. Such early visitors demonstrated the clout that the Woman's Club members held in activist and social reform circles. These speakers, in addition to the members' activity in the community, spurred the Club to action and drove their decision to pursue reforms. The Club did not make decisions in isolation; rather, members reached out and filled needs and gaps that were rapidly growing as the conditions in society changed. Their actions were practical and calculated, and they never wasted a moment on fleeting interests; instead they recognized their strengths and focused their activities where they felt they could make the biggest impact.

In addition to formal meetings and programs, the women convened socially. The Social Committee held receptions for new members, and meetings featured social tea hours and music. Often misunderstood as merely gossip-filled afternoons, these social events contributed greatly to the growth of the Club. It was through these informal discussions in a supportive environment that the ideas for Club work began and moved forward. It was, after all, a gathering over tea that set the stage for this historic story.

Maximum Impact through Collaborations

More and more the clubwomen come to see that our organizations are not so much for self-culture, as to wield the power and the influence which result from union.

—Avis Grant
President, 1909–1911
Chair of the Building Committee

In order to establish themselves in the landscape, the women reached out across the state and also nationally to form connections and exchange ideas with other women. The Club joined the General Federation of Women's Clubs (GFWC) in 1892 after having attended two of the GFWC's conventions, in Chicago and Philadelphia, but dropped its membership in 1901. Meeting minutes hint at a disagreement between the Club and the GFWC on a particular suffrage bill. The Club rejoined the GFWC in 1914.

As early as 1898, the Club engaged in "Reciprocity Days" with other clubs around Illinois where they gathered to collaborate and discuss pressing issues. A Fellowship Day was held even earlier, on September 18, 1896, during which letters from other groups were read, as evidenced by an announcement card in the Club's scrapbook. During the first decades of the 1900s, the Club became more involved in the Tenth District of the Illinois Federation of Women's Clubs, comprised of clubs from the North Shore and north side of Chicago, including Rogers Park, Ravenswood, Edgewater, Winnetka, and Wilmette. The Illinois Federation itself was created in 1894, with the Woman's Club of Evanston being one of the first organizations to join. Based on the needs of their communities, these clubs all pursued essentially the same issues of education, health, economy, crime, and rehabilitation. None of the clubs worked in isolation but rather were all part of a larger movement of the Progressive Era. Networking, connections, and relationships among women all over the city and country led to more successful reforms with a much bigger impact than any one woman or club could have accomplished on their own.

The Club's rapidly growing membership also required more effective communication between members, so the first issue of a monthly newsletter called the *Bulletin* was published in October 1911 after the Bowman Publishing Company agreed to print it at a rate of $7.75 per month. Clifton called the *Bulletin* "essential" in the years before the clubhouse, "because it kept Club members informed of our next meeting place." After a brief hiatus from 1913 to 1915, the *Bulletin* was reinstated and continues to be produced to this day. The pages of the *Bulletin* document the Club's rich history, which would otherwise have received "only a superficial view obtained from newspaper publicity." Filled with reports of Club activities, essays by members, speeches given by famous individuals, photographs of the women and Club events, and advertisements from local businesses, the *Bulletin* not only illustrates the Club's work, but also reveals aspects of the society in which it functioned.

While the *Bulletin*, constitution, and Club motto provided cohesiveness, other features were incorporated to increase solidarity among the women. During the February 14, 1898, board meeting, it was recommended that a Club registry, pledge, color, and pin be adopted, and so an emblem was created in 1917 by Belle Sloane Fowler. In 1899, the Club began to sell pins that members wore to demonstrate visually their connection and unity.

Forming connections within the organization and building collective knowledge strengthened the voices of these women reformers. As social service organizations were becoming more solidified in communities all over the nation, the participation of local women's clubs was contributing greatly to other social service organizations' growth.

Making a Difference

We were a serious group in those days, nothing so frivolous as having our pictures taken ever occurred to us and we never thought of giving bridge parties for revenue.

—Emma Webster
President, 1904–1906

Many women's clubs were initially formed for literary study, and the Woman's Club of Evanston was no exception. Some clubs were content to remain solely literary in nature, particularly those whose membership was made up of women without much formal education. Many members of the Woman's Club of Evanston, however, were well-educated, and while the Club maintained its interest in literature and the arts and humanities, its activities very quickly evolved into philanthropy and service.

Community Health Initiatives

As protectors of the home, women sought to ensure that all individuals had a chance to live healthy, safe lives, and they went about this by creating programs and working to reform social, legal, and health systems even though they were not able to vote. Following the Woman's Club of Evanston's first acts of charity—providing toys to children in need—the Club turned its attention toward creating sustainable organizations in the community. Evanston experienced an outbreak of typhoid fever in 1891, and at that time, the journey into Chicago to see a physician took longer than an ill body could handle. In November of that year, Club member Rebecca Butler, who belonged to the Benevolent Society of Evanston, spoke to the Club about the need to establish "an Emergency Hospital in the village," citing as proof many distressing cases. Butler's presentation spurred the Woman's Club to form a Hospital Committee in March 1892 under the direction of Kate Hubbart. Zimmerman, in "Reminiscences," recalled saying to the women, "Now ladies, as we are an aggregation of women from all the churches or from no church, it seems to me it belongs to us to do this." She explained that "the women of those days were pretty timid," but once the typhoid epidemic grew and the Benevolent Society became "swamped with its work," the Club decided it must raise money to build a hospital.

The Hospital Committee organized a kermess on the third floor of Evanston City Hall during the third week of October. This carnival-like event featured various cultural booths and entertainment, and souvenir programs were sold. The *Fiftieth Anniversary* booklet noted: "Young ladies who were graceful dancers and others who could act and do other interesting things were found to be available, and Evanston society took hold with hearty good will." It goes on to say: "there was plenty of talent in our city to draw upon—singers, dancers and monolinguists. The women sewed, embroidered and painted wares for sale and the merchants were very generous. Boxes overlooking the stage for the performance were sold for as high as fifty dollars." The party was called a "huge success" and a "brilliant social affair." The admission fees brought in $4,183.05, and accounts indicate that $3,600 was given to the hospital fund. The money was given in two installments and earmarked to create a cottage on the premises of the home slated to become the hospital, first located at 806 Emerson Street, to be used specifically for infectious diseases. The cottage was never built, but the money was a significant contribution to the establishment of the hospital overall, according to the Hospital Committee's minutes over the years. Eighteen years later, in 1910, the Club solidified its financial commitment to the hospital when it voted to give one-tenth of its annual income from dues to charity.

Several years later, the Club hired a visiting nurse to care for those who were too sick to leave home or unable to afford a hospital stay. Thus, the

Visiting Nurse Association was created in 1897 with the help of Woman's Club members. Fannie Faltz, the first visiting nurse, made her rounds by bicycle, making in some years thousands of house calls; in 1900, she logged 2,893 visits. As early as December 1897, according to the minutes for the Philanthropy and Sociology Committee, Stanwood invited Club members to her home, for a sewing meeting, "the object being to supply needed materials for the visiting nurse." Sewing became an annual all-Club event in 1911–1912, and the Welfare Sewing Committee (which changed names often in the early years) continued to support various causes for decades. The 1911 board minutes record that "these [sewing] meetings were also very pleasant social gatherings." Parties and other events were held to raise money for the Visiting Nurse Association; for example, $300 was raised in 1898 through a benefit concert. The Woman's Club of Evanston and the Visiting Nurse Association worked closely together in those first founding decades, and the association still exists today under the name of Evanston Northwestern Health Home Services. The Club continued to support the organization until 1997, when it merged with Evanston Hospital.

Visiting Nurse

Sewing Committee

The Club did not take a prominent stand on temperance (also considered a health issue), but its association with Willard and presentations on the issue demonstrate that they supported these efforts. In 1897, upon Harbert's resignation as president of the Woman's Club, the members purchased a drinking fountain in her honor for the Chicago Commons settlement house. Placed at the corner of Milwaukee Avenue and Union Street, with an inscription from the Club to Mrs. Harbert, this fountain was designed to keep people out of saloons, as these were often the only places people could go for a drink of clean water. A publication from the Chicago Commons states: "The drinking fountain presented to the set-

Evanston Hospital

Drinking fountain in honor of Elizabeth Boynton Harbert

tlement by the Evanston Woman's Club is a continuous godsend to the thousands who pass by on Milwaukee Avenue on the hot days, and it saves no insignificant sum in beer money during a year."

These health reform efforts coincided with increasing knowledge about bacteriology, sanitation, cleanliness, and the prevention of disease. Early on, the Club began advocating for a milk inspection station in Evanston. As early as 1900, the Child and Home Department heard a talk from Dr. R. H. Babcock entitled "Some Facts Regarding Tuberculosis Which Mothers Should Know," which warned the women to "beware of your neighbor's cow" because its milk may be spreading tuberculosis. A Milk Committee was formed in 1902 to inspect dairies in Evanston, and four years later the Club asked each member to contribute ten cents to pay a milk inspector from November 1, 1906, to January 1, 1907, with the inspector reporting to the Club. After hearing a talk by health officer Dr. Parkes in 1907, in which he indicated that all but two of the 125 cases of scarlet fever in Evanston were a result of tainted milk, the Club asked the city council to give Parkes $500 to continue tests through the summer. In 1910 Dr. William Evans, health commissioner for Chicago, stated that half of the six thousand deaths of infants in Chicago were caused by impure milk, which prompted the women to encourage the city to establish a permanent bacteriology lab in Evanston. They also asked women with automobiles to inspect dairies around Evanston.

The Club worked to prevent the spread of disease in several other ways. For example, in 1910, the Philanthropy and Sociology Department passed a resolution supporting open-air schoolrooms and medical inspection in Public School Districts 75 and 76. Open-air school rooms were part of a wider open-air movement whose proponents thought to prevent the spread of disease and, in some cases, alleviate symptoms by providing more space to breathe and move (running counter to the crowded slums where disease was prevalent), while medical inspection further helped to curb the spread of disease. The Child and Home Department took a particular interest in the cleanliness of vacant lots and alleys and ensured that garbage was picked up regularly and refuse was cleared from citizens' yards, especially during construction. The women examined the city ordinances on January 10, 1902, and found them to be sufficient but advised the chief of police to distribute educational circulars. By October 1910, Club members decided the ordinances were outdated and encouraged the city council to revise them. Finding that citizens were partly to blame for the city's cleanliness problems, the women advocated for "instructive inspection" and "a campaign of education in civic cleanliness." These broader efforts to keep Evanston's citizens healthy through sanitation and civics education became an intense focus of the Club leading up to World War I.

The women also supported beautification of Evanston. In 1902, they launched a Tree Labeling Committee to examine a project for labeling trees and shrubs in Evanston with their scientific names. They also applauded the city council for its removal of advertisements at elevated train stations in 1903, formed a committee on weeds and poison ivy in 1907, and heard the mayor speak on "Beautifying Evanston" in 1909. In

1910 the Club launched an investigation when billboards appeared once again at the stations. The Club also led a successful campaign to plant the first tree in the new Lake Shore Park at the foot of Greenwood Street in 1911.

Educating the Children

As mothers, Club members felt that they had the best ability and expertise to speak on matters of raising and educating children. By the time the Woman's Club was formed in 1889, the kindergarten movement was well under way nationally and even more so in Chicago. The women heard talks from professionals in the field, including Alice Putnam, who founded the first private kindergarten in Chicago in 1874, and Elizabeth Harrison, who with Putnam founded the Chicago Kindergarten Club in 1883. It was later renamed the Chicago Kindergarten Training College and eventually became part of National Louis University. In Evanston, kindergartens were created to serve the growing population and to embrace this new development in early childhood education. In 1894, the Woman's Club gave $25 to support a free kindergarten in Evanston, which was likely the idea of Mary Willard, sister-in-law of Frances Willard. Before that, the Club had donated $150 to the kindergarten at the Northwestern University Settlement House. The settlement house was founded by the university's tenth president, Henry Wade Rogers, and his wife, Emma, a charter member of the Woman's Club and a vice president from 1891 to 1894. Katherine Beebe, the first public school kindergarten teacher in Evanston (located at Dewey School) was also a very active member of the Woman's Club, no doubt influencing the Club's connection with teachers generally.

The women fought for laws regarding educational standards, requirements, and teacher training. In 1892, Stanwood, the Club's second president, was the first woman elected to the District 75 school board, making her also the first woman elected to a public office in Evanston in one of the first elections in which women could vote in Illinois. In March 1896, Stanwood attended a meeting about teacher training legislation at the Leland Hotel in Chicago. The next year, she and Kate McMullen served as delegates to the first National Congress of Mothers convention in Washington, DC, which no doubt strengthened Stanwood's desire to pursue this work in the community alongside her duties as the mother of three children. One of her children went with her to the convention: "I, with my small, three-year-old girl tucked under my arm, went with Mrs. McMullen because I . . . had to take care of my children." She went on, in "Reminiscences," to explain her feelings at this event: "To see mothers from California to Maine drawn together just for no other reason than that they were mothers was a wonderful thing. And the funny thing about it was that there were as many spinsters as there were real mothers. But, you know, there are mothers by the grace of God as well as mothers by the physical process, and I don't doubt that they were all just as much mothers." Stanwood urged the Woman's Club's to continue its membership in the Illinois Society for Child Study. In the 1890s, women's clubs often affiliated with other organizations to cross-pollinate ideas and ideologies. Stanwood helped organize the Illinois Congress of Mothers, a predecessor to the PTA. ISCS was founded in May 1894 and served as a model for other states; its annual summer conferences attracting large audiences. Stanwood also served as chairwoman of the Legislation Committee of the National Congress of Mothers in 1900 and as president of the Illinois Federation of Women's Clubs from 1900 to 1902. At her urging, the Club provided funds to implement vision and hearing tests in Evanston schools starting in 1897.

Kate McMullen also played a prominent role in establishing connections between mothers and teachers. A charter member, she served on the Club's Finance Committee in 1894–95, as chair of the Child and Home Department and a member of the Programs Committee in 1898–99, and on the Board of Directors in 1902–1903. After attending the National Congress of Mothers with Stanwood in 1897, she attended again in 1898, 1899, and 1900. "I never saw a flower bud under the influence of the sun as I saw dear Mrs. McMullen's soul expand and open and blossom in that Mothers' Congress," Stanwood said of her colleague.

> Her children had come fast, and her home life was bound up in that little home circle. All at once she went to this great big place, and she was so modest and so timid and so frightened that I didn't believe she could stand up in her own parlor and talk to three or four of us without fainting dead away, and here she was ready and willing to

talk about this Mothers' Congress in front of our Woman's Club. I know I sat back and reveled. She hesitated and faltered, but she was always after just the right word.

McMullen served as vice president of the Illinois Society for Child-Study in 1900, as well as a founder and first president of the Illinois Congress of Mothers in 1900. Inspired by her previous participation in the National Congress of Mothers, she called together clubwomen from all over the state to Evanston's Emanuel Methodist Church to hear speakers on the topic of parent-teacher cooperation. The Woman's Club served lunch to more than three hundred guests, with $135 allotted for this purpose, and thirteen loaves of cake provided by board members. This marked the start of the Illinois Parent-Teacher Association (PTA). Despite being criticized for leaving her husband "helplessly at home" with the children while she traveled, McMullen felt that her role as a mother inspired her to make conditions better for *all* children. She also pursued work in compulsory education, the juvenile court, and restricted child labor.

Rather than simply directing teachers, the women talked with them to learn about their projects and concerns. An article in the Club's scrapbook and its calendar mention that after a presentation in November 1896, Katherine Beebe "succeeded in leaving an impression that there were still some who were in need of books and clothing." In response, Emma Moore created the Mother's Club of Noyes Street, the first mother's club in Evanston, the next year. The Woman's Club bought a knitting machine in 1897 for the group to knit garments for children in need at the school. In 1901, the Club began to invite teachers to all of its meetings and honored teachers with receptions in 1889 and again in 1906. In February 1902, the Club received twenty tickets through the Municipal Art League of Chicago to attend the art galleries of Bertha Palmer, a prominent member of the Chicago Woman's Club. Ten tickets were allotted to the Art and Literature Department, and the Club gave the other ten to teachers of Evanston.

In addition to building relationships with teachers, the women worked to include particular subjects in public school curricula. In 1894, Alice Stockham, Kingsley, and Harbert formed the Household Economics Committee for the purpose of adding domestic science training to the curriculum in the local public schools—a goal that was not immediately realized. The first facilities for domestic science education in Evanston were located at Haven School, and in 1901, the Club staged an operetta and raised $400 to purchase utensils and other equipment for the program. The women believed that giving children these domestic science skills early would allow them to find work in the hospitality field and also practice better management at home, which was part of a larger push for the Americanization and assimilation of newly arrived immigrants. The Philanthropy and Sociology Department also sought to integrate playgrounds and civics courses into the everyday school curriculum so that children could develop their life skills through both playful and practical activity.

Furthering their drive to give children access to education, the Woman's Club supported the idea of traveling libraries that would deliver books around the city and out to rural areas. In 1900, after hearing a talk on the subject by Katherine Sharp, director of the library school at the Armour Institute in Chicago, the Club contributed $50 and donated seventy-six books to create a traveling library, which was first sent to Glenview. By October 1902, twenty-five libraries had been sent out. The minutes of the Child and Home Department state: "the amount of good done by good books is beyond estimation and their influence on future genera-

Evanston Traveling Library

tions untold," and further that the Club was the first in the state to send out a rural traveling library.

The women also supported the opening of children's reading rooms in Chicago Public Libraries and a new free public library in Evanston in early 1903. At the time, libraries were rudimentary, book depositories with very few of the kinds of spaces and services we take for granted in a public library today. To have rooms specifically devoted to children's books was novel. Charles McNeill Grey, mayor of Chicago 1853–1854, had pledged $100,000 if Evanston could raise another $50,000. In response, the Woman's Club formed a committee, led by Ellen Wyman, to canvass the town, seeking pledges and meeting with groups such as the University Guild, the Fortnightly Club, and the Bryant Club. In the Executive Committee minutes, it was noted that "Mrs. Harbert emphasized the fact that the library was so largely used by women and children that it was fitting that the former should assist this movement." The women raised $30,000, which fell short of the amount the town needed. However, their commitment to libraries continued, and in 1905, they wrote letters to their legislators supporting a Library Extension Bill to promote the creation of free libraries around the state.

The Philanthropy and Sociology Department worked on issues specifically related to orphans, juvenile offenders, and working women — groups they believed were particularly vulnerable. In 1899, the Cook County Juvenile Court was established as the first juvenile court in the nation. Its purpose was to remove young people from the penal system and place them in centers where they could be rehabilitated. In 1901, Edna Sheldrake, a probation officer of the Chicago Juvenile Court, inspired the Club to raise hundreds of dollars the following year to retain a probation officer — Susan Clark of the Chicago Juvenile Court — to carry out work in Evanston. That year, Clark reported that seven children in Evanston had been helped with her services. Also in 1902, the women supported a Compulsory Education Bill requiring children age seven to fourteen to attend school in an attempt to curb both truancy and child labor. The Club formed a Probation Work Committee in 1908, which introduced Edith Ennis and Irma Hotchkiss as volunteer probation officers. Ennis "gave a graphic account of the work which occupies her time," having reported that 165 children in Evanston needed care, while eighteen were on parole. Ennis joined the Woman's Club that year and served as president from 1921 to 1923. She was instrumental in Club work for social services to juveniles—for example, raising money for a YMCA after-school program for boys under sixteen at Haven School and aiding in the appointment of a female policewoman at the jail. According to the Philanthropy and Sociology Department minutes for March 2, 1908, girls in jail could be subject to abuses by male police officers. The Club supported the efforts of Ennis and Hotchkiss until a paid probation officer was hired.

The women supported a number of young adult programs attended by children in the juvenile court system at recreation and rehabilitation centers and schools all over the north side of Chicago. As an example, after the Philanthropy and Sociology Department heard a report from Chandler in 1904 about a parental school (boarding schools acting in the place of parents) in Bowmanville that cared for more than two hundred boys, the women sent books, magazines, and paper for the boys to use. This support grew over the years; for example, according the October 2, 1905, minutes, $102 was sent to the Adams Street School. The Club's Vacation Schools Committee, operating from 1900 to 1909 to provide a form of summer school, pledged $30 to help cover the cost of boys' membership at the YMCA. In this first decade of the century, the Club put thousands of dollars and many hours of time toward rehabilitation work with juveniles.

Women and Girls First

The women of the Philanthropy and Sociology Department (which changed its name to the Social Service Department in 1911) took an especially active interest in the status of immigrant and working girls and young women. During 1902–1903, a Legislative Committee was formed within this department to gather information about issues such as the legal status of these women. They heard numerous presentations by the YWCA Traveler's Aid Committee, which worked to "look after and protect the innocent unsuspecting and friendless girls as they enter the city, and offer escape to them from the many varied and plausible devices which beset them to lure them down to a life of shame." For its support the Club received a certificate of membership in this association in 1927, demonstrating the members' long-standing commitment to protecting the city's most vulnerable. The women also endeavored to raise wages for working women, as it was feared they would seek "cheap" and thus inappropriate amusements: "With a weekly wage of $4, how can a girl remain pure and yet support herself?" Catherine Waugh McCulloch spoke heavily in support of an age of consent law, advocating that it be raised from fourteen to eighteen; in 1905, the Club sent fifty-six letters to the clergy and presidents of the various societies and Clubs in Evanston, asking them to sign a petition in support of this law, and 623 signatures were forwarded to the state legislature in Springfield.

The women also took up work with destitute mothers. In 1908, the minutes of the Philanthropy and Sociology Department notes that members were asked to visit newly incarcerated women and children in jail to offer "advice and sympathy." The Club also held discussions considering welfare or pensions for these women. After Jane Zimmerman led a discussion on the topic, news that the Club was engaged in this work made it all the way onto the back of a theater program in New York. *Success Magazine* had contacted Zimmerman about writing an article about this topic. Later, she recalled that just as she "was putting the finishing touches to my article . . . the evening paper was brought in with President Roosevelt's address to Congress, in which he recommended 'Pensions for Destitute Mothers.' He must have seen the back of that same theater program. Within a few weeks, *Success Magazine* sent back my article. President Roosevelt had stolen the thunder."

In January 1908, Elizabeth Odell spoke about the Illinois Industrial School for Girls, which had been started in Evanston in 1877 and provided housing and job training to orphaned and delinquent girls. Originally located at Sheridan and Main in Evanston, the school moved to Park Ridge in 1908 and was renamed the Park Ridge School for Girls. In 1909, the women pledged $25 to the school to furnish a room and gave another $50 in 1911. The women held several parties for the girls, complete with gifts, food, and other entertainment, and they also supported the school's Flower Mission, which collected flowers for the girls to sell in Chicago to gain skills and earn money.

The Club contributed $25 to the Illinois Children's Home and Aid Society in 1908, and in 1909 gave $17.50 to the Sarah Hackett Stevenson Memorial Lodging House for Women, which provided housing for thirty-five women looking for work. In 1910, Zimmerman put out a call for rags so that members could weave rugs for the women residents. In 1911, the women pledged money to Gad's Hill, which held a summer camp for impoverished mothers and their children.

The Club also focused on working women's concerns. In 1899, in an item found in the Club's scrapbook, McMullen announced the opening of a free day nursery—"for the benefit of mothers who have to work and to whom the care of their babies has been a serious problem"—with the help of the "philanthropic gentlemen" of the Emmanuel Methodist Church. The nursery was an outgrowth of the work of Fannie Faltz, the visiting nurse whom the Club appointed and paid. Later, the Woman's Club sponsored programs at the Evanston Day Nursery, including a Christmas party for the children in 1912.

Influencing Working Conditions

The women of the Club took an active interest in labor conditions, supporting child labor bills and the work of the truancy officer Helen Jewel, so that children would go to school and get an education rather than fall victim to harsh factory working conditions. They fought to give clerks in the city of Evanston a half holiday each Wednesday, even threatening to boycott businesses that did not comply. They heard presentations on the employability of fathers released from jail and on safety issues at work.

Under the leadership of the Child and Home Department, the women also sought to teach employable domestic science skills to adult learners. In 1894, the Club gave $40 to the Benevolent Society for a dressmaking class and $14 to the Society of Associated Charities to purchase systems (sewing machines and equipment) for their sewing class. They held a series of dressmaking classes for women of the community in 1901. Starting in 1904, members organized domestic science exhibits and competitions for community domestic workers and students in the public schools, awarding prizes for "gelatin or cornstarch dessert," "breakfast rolls," and "potato salad." In 1903, Anna Rew Gross convinced the Club to create a household register that helped women find jobs in domestic service. For many years, the Club awarded a scholarship to a local girl to attend the Chicago School of Domestic Arts and Science. Through these efforts, the women sought to teach employable skills to women and children, improve morale among workers, and increase efficiency and productivity in their own homes.

Domestic Arts and Science

The interest in domestic science coincided with increased interest in municipal ordinances and involvement in civic matters. It also demonstrated a growing awareness of the connection between efficient work in the home, nutrition, and the conservation of resources, which would become especially applicable during World War I. Foreshadowing this event, the Child and Home Department learned about Jorinne Turner's "eggless, butterless, milkless cake" in November 1912, and it was decided that, during this time, "ten minutes of every meeting be spent in exchange of household items of interest." The women's increased personal interest in domestic matters reflects the price of their success. Women, who at one time could be employed only in domestic roles, were heading in droves for better-paying jobs in factories, with better hours and conditions that women's clubs all over the nation had fought for. Domestic help became increasingly scarce, and the women of Evanston who had previously employed others quickly had to learn how to do some of these domestic tasks themselves, or else they had to learn how to increase the efficiency of the few servants that remained.

The Club began holding domestic science courses in October 1903, with the first in a series given by Lynn Boyd of the Evanston Manual Training College on the subject of Chinese domestic science. These courses were free to Club members and offered to nonmembers at $2.50 for a series of nine lectures or fifty cents for a single lecture. The women were also encouraged to attend courses and lectures at the Chicago School of Domestic Arts and Science.

Cultural Studies

Despite the Club's strong commitment to social services reform, art, literary, and cultural studies were the true foundation of the Club and helped women to educate themselves on a level that they felt would bring them respect. In the minutes for the general meeting in 1890, we find this statement:

> The foremost idea in the minds of the [Art and Literature]
> committee being to show to the world the wonderful

development in the education of women there has
been in the last-quarter of a century. Women have been
working along with admirable vigor very close to the
leaders of masculine art; the women are coming up the
slope reaching for the highest places—if not the highest,
certainly what is far better, to be side by side. The time is
at hand for women of lofty imagination, breadth of vision,
and depth of insight to lay out their work so that it will
have a powerful influence upon civilization.

Education in the humanities also allowed them to develop their
research, writing, and public speaking skills, which they could apply to
their reform activities. Even more important, through arts and letters the
women studied yet another dimension of the human condition, which
contributed to their knowledge of morals and behavior.

The Art and Literature Department of the Woman's Club began in
1892 as the World's Fair Committee. In the years before and during the
World's Columbian Exposition of 1893 in Chicago, the women welcomed guests who highlighted the role of women at the event. In one
instance, 161 women gathered at Harbert's home to hear Bertha Palmer
speak on women's work for the World's Fair. According to Stanwood's
Club history, Elizabeth Cady Stanton had written to Harbert asking for
the Club's help in ensuring a clean city for the fair.

The Art and Literature Department remained popular long after the
world's fair had ended, and the Club created new departments to meet
the members' expanding interests. Music and French Departments were
created in 1897 and became classes soon after. Until 1900, the departments chose a study theme each year; for example, the study of French
provinces was a focus in 1897–1898.

Suffrage: A Neutral Position

Although Harbert and other members were suffrage activists, the Club
never took up women's voting rights as a main focus. In the Club's
archives for 1891, Alice Moseley explains that the women drew their
strength from the diversity of interests and viewpoints of the members,

and indeed, not all Club members supported women's suffrage. A 1912 article in the *Evanston Daily News* notes that "Mrs. Charles Clifton, President of the Evanston Woman's Club, was questioned as to her attitude on equal suffrage. She replied that she was quite indifferent to it, if anything, opposed." By contrast, Edith Ennis was in favor of suffrage, stating, "more and more purposeful people are coming to see in the extension of suffrage to women an opportunity for union in action which will work toward a more speedy solution of at least some of our many perplexing social problems."

The Club's interest in suffrage centered on support of certain legislation, invitations to select speakers, and events such as a reception for Susan B. Anthony at Harbert's home. In 1908, the board recommended endorsing a resolution asking the National Republican Committee to include a measure giving women equal voting rights as men, and two delegates were sent to the committee meeting. In 1909, the Club sent a delegate to Springfield for a hearing on municipal suffrage for women. The Club's reluctance to take a stand on suffrage as an organization may have stemmed from the possibility of being barred from entering other public spheres where they could quickly enact change. In the *Fiftieth Anniversary* booklet, in a section commenting on the early years of the *Bulletin*, the authors looked back and observed that "we see much written [in the *Bulletin*] for uplifting the cause of women, but no word of 'Votes for Women' which cause at that time was shaking the country. As late as 1918 it was considered, if not absolutely indecorous, at least inexpedient to mention so controversial a subject in the club. With politics, Woman's Suffrage was taboo."

The Club did often discuss legal issues, such as equal wages for women and the protection of children, and in 1902–1903 they held a twice-monthly "civics" class to educate themselves in the ways of government. Without the vote, the women wrote letters to their legislators and did whatever else they could to get reforms passed.

Spearheading this effort was Catherine Waugh McCulloch, a lawyer and women's rights activist. In 1907, she created the Club's Legislative Committee to educate members on various legal issues and bills under consideration at state and local levels. During the 1907–1908 year, McCulloch spoke on eight different bills, including one to raise the age of consent for children, a bill on joint guardianship of children, a wife desertion bill, and even a "Chicago Municipal Suffrage" bill. During the 1912–1913 year, McCulloch held an "experimental" civics class to learn more about these issues. Although the Club may not have directly addressed suffrage as an organization, the members' work for smaller, community-based changes improved the status of women and set the stage for the passage of suffrage in Illinois in 1913 and national suffrage in 1920.

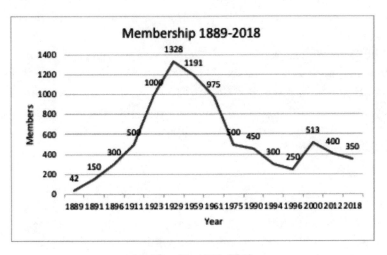

Membership 1889–2018

A Home of Our Own

Membership requirements became stricter as interest in the Club increased. By 1900, a potential member had to be nominated by three members. Members could nominate one person per year once they had been members themselves for two years. Each prospective member also had to submit her qualifications, which likely included her social status, affiliations, and her ability to contribute, to be voted on by the board. Despite these restrictions, the waiting list and member roster grew each year, and in 1902, the Club decided to extend associate memberships to those living within a five-mile radius of Evanston.

This immense increase in membership prompted the Club to move meetings from private homes to various meeting spaces. During what

Ellen Wyman, in the *Fortieth Anniversary* booklet, called the "Moving Period," the Club met at such places as Odd Fellows Hall, the Country Club, and the Boat Club. "When the Club was organized by that wonderful Mother of us all, Mrs. Elizabeth Boynton Harbert," Wyman wrote in the *Fortieth Anniversary* booklet, "it was sheltered and nurtured in her own home. . . . Then came the time when it should step out, assert its own individuality and assume responsibility. Friends and neighbors extended hands of fellowship and welcomed the young club with open doors." In many of these places, in lieu of rent or a fee paid, the Club offered works of art or furniture such as chairs.

Recognizing the need for a permanent meeting space, the Club formed a temporary building committee in 1892, made up of women from different churches so as to reach a wider audience. Six women were designated to canvass the town, seeking suitable spaces.

Not everyone agreed on the need for a clubhouse. "There was a general response, but a wide divergence of opinion," explained Emma Webster, in "Reminiscences of 30 Years," a document encompassing memories of the Club's oldest members. "Some people thought women's clubs had reached the apex of achievement; others thought if women bothered themselves with a building, it would cause them no end of trouble. Some thought we ought to have it, but we ought to have it at as small an outlay as possible; but others thought we should go to work and build a good building."

A permanent building committee was finally created in April 1894. Several opportunities to build presented themselves, but each was voted down due to location and cost. Harbert suggested the Club look at the lot on the southwest corner of Orrington and Church, but the Club now faced the issue of incorporation. Without legal recognition, raising money would be nearly impossible. The Club was incorporated on March 10, 1898, which firmly established it as a serious organization and also enabled it to sell stocks and bonds and raise money for a clubhouse through subscription. Incorporation, however, came shortly after a time of transition, marked by Harbert's resignation as president in 1897.

While the Club was considering lots for a clubhouse, the Evanston YMCA building at 1611-21 Orrington Avenue was completed, and the Club began to rent rooms there in 1898. In "Reminiscences of 30 Years," Webster hinted that they were not wanted there. The Club paid $50 a month to lease the rooms at all times, not just for meetings and events, and this allowed the Club to sublet its rooms to other organizations and individuals as a means of generating income. With $500 from the Rooms Committee, allotted in 1898, members began furnishing the rooms at the Y, and they continued to replace curtains, draperies, rugs, and other furniture as needed. In January 1906, the women voted to set aside money annually for art, presumably to hang in the Club's rooms. Nellie Kingsley, looking back, exclaimed, "I remember at the time, we disliked very much to pay so much for a picture—$25!" Except for a year spent at St. Mark's Parish (1907–1908), the Club rented rooms at the YMCA until 1912. That year, they held meetings in churches around Evanston in anticipation of the completion of their clubhouse.

The building sinking fund to build a clubhouse was annulled in October 1897, shortly after securing rooms at the YMCA. When the women revisited the idea of a clubhouse fifteen years after the first attempt, they envisioned a meeting space that would be open to all residents, promoting a sense of community and contributing greatly to civic and aesthetic life in Evanston.

The community showed interest in the women's efforts, as announced in the *Evanston Index*, November 5, 1910:

> On all sides was heard the same advice—"build something we all can be proud of," "Consider the future of the town as well as of the Club," "Build on a corner, not on an inside lot." Other Clubs desiring the use of the hall, teachers wishing to give musicales or entertainments, young people who hope to use the hall for dances, citizens interested in better things for Evanston and desiring a hall for civic meetings, all urged the Club to greater effort.

The women of the Club wanted to hold lectures, concerts, plays, banquets, and bazaars in both their large and small auditoriums, and they were also focused on the building as a center for young people to hold dances so that they would not have to go out of town or to unsafe spaces to have their events. The large auditorium was originally to be located on the ground level, but members objected to the square footage it would require, and discussion over this issue delayed the project. The Building

Committee noted that placing the auditorium on the second floor would provide unexpected space on the first floor and "proved so adaptable to our needs and desires" that the revised plan was then quickly passed. The members wanted their auditorium to "supply the Club itself with a meeting place not too large for a woman's voice." The Club also required that "the hall should also be constructed with reference to its acoustic qualities, that a woman's voice can be easily heard in every part." Smaller rooms would accommodate groups and committees wishing to hold meetings, and a kitchen would allow for luncheons and banquets for the Club and other organizations. By renting space in the clubhouse, the Club could generate income and become more independent.

A Ways and Means Committee, chaired by Ida C. Cook, was appointed in February 1910 to investigate the possibilities of establishing a building fund. A Building Committee was formed with Avis Grant as the chair. By April of that year, the Club voted to purchase the lot located on the northwest corner of Davis Street and Chicago Avenue from Marie Kidder, a longtime resident of Evanston, for $8,000. Only a few months later, the women decided to exchange this lot and pay an additional $4,000 for a more desirable one located only a block north, on the northwest corner of Chicago Avenue and Church Street. Ernest Mayo, a favored architect in Evanston and throughout the entire North Shore, was approved as the architect for the clubhouse in January 1911. The famous architectural firm of Holabird and Roche acted as advice and counsel.

As the building was to be a center for the community, the community was asked to contribute to its construction, promoting a sense of connection and togetherness. In a "never-to-be-forgotten whirlwind campaign," the Club solicited both cash and certificate subscriptions from the members. Certificate subscriptions allowed donors to pledge a specific amount and pay in installments twice a year for five years. After Club members had raised $8,000, the women canvassed the community to raise the balance. An announcement from Helen Dawes and Ann Elisabeth Bass read, "Fifty loyal members of the Club have volunteered the task of canvassing, in pairs, all the big hearted men of Evanston. It will be embarrassing work for them. So, please make it as easy as you can for the two members who will call on you." Harriet Clifton, president at the time of the cornerstone laying and grand opening, opined that it also brought the members closer together. "It was a good thing for the Club that we had to inveigle our friends into parting with their worldly goods for the sake of our new building, because it kept us awake and pepped us up—we had to work together, and together we worked—everything and everybody. A united group with a determined spirit."

Soon, the women had raised an additional $14,000 from the community. At a church bazaar at the First Methodist Church, Avis Grant bravely approached philanthropist James A. Patten about a donation. She later wrote, "We were grouped at different tables, and I was to sit at a certain table. I discovered that I was placed at a long table at the other end of which was Mr. Patten's place card. I didn't say a word to anybody, but just took the place card of the person sitting next to Mr. Patten, and put my own in its place. I just had to!" He graciously offered a third of the building costs, "just like that!" He agreed to this percentage even after Grant was "almost embarrassed" to "give him the itemized statement" which exceeded the original cost by several thousand dollars. This increase in cost, however, may have been Patten's doing in the first place. According to Grant's report, "we would take the plans to Mr. Patten, and he would say 'You ought to have a bigger room than that.' Really, he had more of a men's Club in view than we did, but then he said he wanted a good one, and he wanted a big one, and finally when we had our bids, and found it was going to cost $54,000, we submitted them again to Mr. Patten, and he said, 'Go ahead!'" Norma Stearns later recalled that Grant would "recount [the story] with glee still evident in her sparkling eyes."

Money raised from department classes and fundraisers went to the building fund, and the Club held a festival at Ravinia Park as well as a bazaar and an opera/dinner, which brought in hundreds of dollars. Businesses all around Evanston also contributed; for example, the *Evanston Index* pledged $1.25 for each newspaper subscription that the women brought in, while the Evanston Commercial Association, Torcom Brothers, Lord's Department Store, and Bowman Publishing Company all made donations or commissions.

As happens with most large-scale building projects, the women soon realized that they had underbudgeted. The project would cost approximately $20,000 more than they had anticipated, so they reluctantly took out a loan from the State Bank of Evanston. The final statement for the

Laying of the cornerstone

building project, dated April 22, 1914, indicates that the building was paid for as follows:

- Cash subscriptions: $23,204.69
- Gift from James A. Patten: $24,500.00
- Proceeds of loans: $25,000.00
- Payments on certificates: $8,068.00
- Funds raised by entertainments: $4,400.57
- Miscellaneous sources, including commissions and interest: $767.55

The cornerstone was laid May 28, 1912, to great fanfare. Sadly, their beloved Mrs. Harbert was ill and unable to attend the ceremony. Her husband, William S. Harbert, came in her place, bringing her good wishes and pride in what the Club had become. He read a telegram she had sent along:

> May the foundations you have so faithfully laid in
> remarkable harmony, love and wisdom, result in a temple
> beautiful, from whose every window shall radiate the
> light of truth, and whose doors, as they have ever done
> for almost a quarter of a century, open quickly into every
> avenue of helpful service for the weak, the invalid, the
> child, the school, the church of the Master, who went
> about doing good, the state and the home.

President Clifton "handled the silver trowel gracefully in adding the finishing touches to the setting of the stone." Both A. W. Harris, president of Northwestern University, and James Patten spoke, with Patten acknowledging that he could "speak only for the men—the ladies can speak for themselves." Clifton emphasized the clubhouse as a center of the community in her speech:

> We, as a Club, are most appreciative and grateful for all
> the assistance which the men and women of this city have
> given us, whether financial or otherwise, and hope that the
> good which can be accomplished through the use of our
> new building, the benefit it can be to the city of Evanston,

will in a slight degree repay the kindness of its citizens. . . .
We are working for the betterment of humanity and that
covers a vast field of labor for it reaches into all lines of
philanthropic and social work.

The clubhouse opened on March 11, 1913, with a party fit for the occasion and twelve thousand people in attendance at this "veritable fairyland." The building was described by the *Lake Shore News* on its front page, as "handsome" and "commodious." In a letter to her niece, preserved in the Club's scrapbook, May Corby reminisced about the party: "I can see them all so beautifully gowned and gracious! With dear departed Mrs. Buswell in such a lovely real lace gown; little Mrs. Streeter in a soft embroidered net—and I—oh, I wore my first and only Drecoll creation of black jet— just the pride of my life." The women involved in the building project, in formal dress, received guests on the second floor, while attendees were free to mill around the clubhouse and especially the auditorium, where orchestra music and an a cappella choir provided entertainment. According to the *Lake Shore News*, "the Club's colors, green and gold, were carried out in the decoration scheme, palms, ferns, and yellow spring flowers being used. The tea room was especially charmingly decorated and was presided over by fifty or more of the ladies, who poured and served coffee to hundreds of guests during the evening. Dainty china of green and gold design, bearing the crest of the Club, was used."

The house had only the finest furnishings, including "carpets from Carson Pirie Scott and Company," while "the stage was decorated as a flower garden, and the Club house was lighted as brilliantly by the smiles of the Club's members as by the new electric fixtures" made of brass. A portrait of Mrs. Harbert painted by Frederick Webster was the first picture hung in the new space. Avis Grant overheard some guests say, "Some receptions are so formal, but this one isn't a bit stiff." A history of the Club written for the fortieth anniversary included this description:

The house never looked more beautiful, brilliantly lighted
and decorated, and the praises sang by those attending
warmed our hearts so that we were fairly bursting with
pride. We had accomplished what three years before had
seemed impossible, we owned our own Club home.

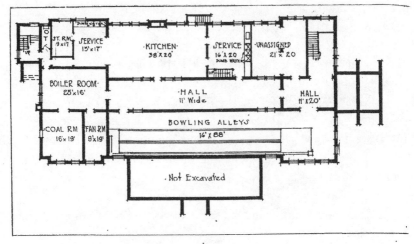

BASEMENT FLOOR

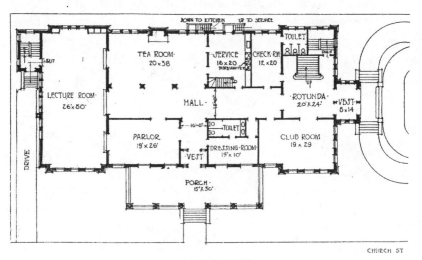

FIRST FLOOR

CHURCH ST

Original blueprints

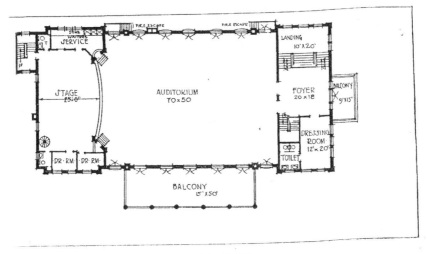

SECOND FLOOR

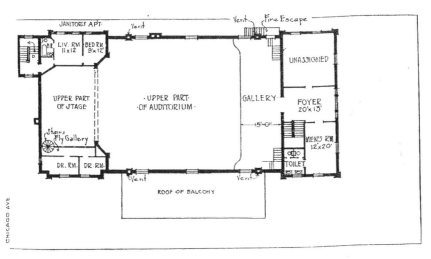

GALLERY FLOOR

Original blueprints

WOMAN'S CLUB NEW BUILDING IS COMPLETED

Finishing Touches Completed on Handsome Structure Which Will Serve As Social Center Here.

RECEPTION TUESDAY EVE

Fourteen Hundred Invitations Sent to Evanstonians to Attend the Initial Function in New Quarters.

The reception which formally opened the new building of the Evanston Woman's club Tuesday evening was one of the greatest, if not the foremost, social success of the season.

The club's colors, green and gold, were carried out in the decoration scheme, palms, ferns and yellow spring flowers being used. The tea room was especially charmingly decorated and was presided over by fifty or more of the ladies, who poured and served coffee to hundreds of guests during the evening. Dainty china of green and gold design, bearing the crest of the club, was used.

Ballroom, view from the balcony

Ballroom, set up for an event

Members' Room

Parlor, now part of the Main Room

Tea Room, 1929

The First Twenty-Five Years

Through its first twenty-four years, the Woman's Club of Evanston contributed to the creation of social service and health organizations, advocated for the passing of city ordinances, and supported laws and bills meant to improve the status of women, children, and the entire fabric of society. The Club had also laid a foundation for themselves by creating a constitution, Club offices, membership rules, and meetings; achieving incorporation; forming connections with other organizations; and holding numerous social events meant to build relationships and enhance cohesiveness. These years were about figuring out what they wanted and how to go about accomplishing that, and they were now welcoming the next generation of clubwomen into their organization. Their work and outreach activities in these first years made them into a strong, permanent, and visible force in the community. These accomplishments could not have come at a more crucial time, as the world would soon encounter the First World War and the Great Depression. The Woman's Club was ready to face these challenges head on.

The Woman's Club of Evanston, circa 1920s

CHAPTER TWO

World War I:
Working from Our New Home

After nearly twenty-five years, the Woman's Club had literally laid a foundation in the community with the construction of their clubhouse in the center of Evanston. During the first years in the building, the Club solidified an enduring place in the community by continuing social service and civic work and expanding and strengthening connections with other organizations.

Our Clubhouse

Taking Care of Business

As planned, the clubhouse became a center for the community. The Club quickly realized that rental schedules and rules needed to be established. Rules included the expected—for example, "furnishings shall not be taken from the premises"—but also the unexpected: no dogs or roller skates allowed in the clubhouse. Evanston's dry status banned "intoxicating drink in any form." "Objectionable dancing" was also prohibited, and the Evening Parties Committee announced: "When the ballroom becomes crowded, it is requested and expected that out of consideration for the other dancers, members and their guests will refrain from dancing eccentric dances." While the women wanted to promote a sociable atmosphere, they also had to maintain the reputation of both the Club *and* the clubhouse.

As promised, the clubhouse also provided a safe space for high school and college students to hold dances and parties, provided at least two chaperones were present at each gathering. After a 1918 investigation into

House Rules

1. The Club House will be open for inspection and use of members from 8 a. m. to 6 p. m. on all days except Sunday.

2. To avoid conflicts all meetings shall be arranged for in advance, either with the chairman of the House Committee or the caretaker of the building.

3. All notices and placards other than Club matter must be approved by the House Committee before they are posted.

4. All notices and placards must be placed on bulletin boards.

5. No decorations shall be affixed to the building or furnishings without specific approval in writing by the House Committee.

6. Members are requested not to reprimand the employes. Should any cause of complaint arise, the attention of the House Committee should be immediately directed thereto.

7. No dog or roller skates shall be allowed in the Club House.

8. All complaints, requests and suggestions as to Club House management shall be made in writing, signed and addressed to the House Committee.

9. No employe of the Club shall be sent on errands off the premises except on urgent Club business.

10. The Club House furnishings shall not be taken from the premises.

11. No member shall give money or any gratuity to any employe of the Club.

12. There shall be no playing of games for money on the Club premises.

13. No petition or subscription papers shall be circulated on the Club premises, unless previously endorsed by the Board of Managers.

14. No tickets except for Club activities shall be offered for sale on the Club premises at the time of Club Meetings.

15. The Club will not be held responsible for articles lost or left on the premises.

Extra copies of the Year Book may be procured for fifty cents.

Rules and Information Concerning Evening Parties

Members will be admitted on presentation of Club tickets for current year.

Members of the family of any Club member will be admitted if introduced in writing by such club member.

Each member will be limited to two guests at a charge of fifty cents per guest.

Guests may be invited as often as desired, but in all cases must be accompanied by a club member or member of her family.

Guests arriving without their hostess will be invited into the club parlor to await her coming.

All guest fees must be paid at the door.

Members are requested *not* to bring children under sixteen years of age.

Tables will be prepared for those who wish to play cards or games.

All suggestions or complaints must be referred to the General Chairman.

MRS. ALICE E. ADAMS, *General Chairman*

House rules, circa 1914

activities at the Bohemian Room, a club in the basement of a confectionary known as the Pink Shop, located at 600 Davis Street, the Parent-Teacher Association asked that the clubhouse be opened for dances on Friday and Saturday afternoons. Worries about the Bohemian Room may have been generational, however. Norma Stearns, President from 1951 to 1953, reminisced: "Perhaps I should not admit it, but I was there once in awhile, as a college student, and I never saw anything devastatingly wrong." Club rules also prohibited its members from selling tickets to other charitable events during social gatherings and prevented businesses and other organizations from using the Club platform to advertise.

Onetime rentals costs were anywhere from $10 for a lecture room with a west entrance to $45 for the second floor auditorium to $60 for the entire house, a fee that had jumped to $75 by 1920. And the rentals caused some headaches. Once, through a misunderstanding, a political organization working to elect a controversial mayoral candidate rented the clubhouse. The candidate installed a rolltop desk, a filing cabinet, telephones, and other office equipment in the clubhouse parlor before the mistake was discovered.

BULLETIN OF THE WOMAN'S CLUB OF EVANSTON [13

Our Club House

In response to many inquiries regarding the rates for rentals of the Club House and its equipment, the House Committee submits the following list, hoping that each club member will carefully preserve it for future reference.

RATES FOR RENTALS

Whole House	$60.00
Auditorium, single rental afternoon or evening	45.00
Auditorium morning, no artificial light	40.00
Auditorium series, 6 or more	35.00
Auditorium series, 12 or more	25.00
Flat rental to students	30.00
Lower Floor	30.00
Lecture Room, single rental	15.00
Lecture Room, single rental, with west entrance	10.00
Lecture Room, 6 or more	10.00
Tea Room, single rental	15.00
Tea Room, 6 or more	10.00
Parlor, single rental	10.00
Parlor, in a series	2.50
Parlor, with Tea or Lecture Room	20.00

KITCHEN AND BOWLING ALLEY

Are included with whole house rental. Serving kitchen on lower floor included with lower floor rental, and stage kitchen with Auditorium.

Kitchen rental	2.50
Bowling Alley	2.50

REHEARSALS

One free rehearsal allowed with each rental of Auditorium for play, concert, etc., at times assigned not to interfere with other rentals.

Extra rehearsals, each	5.00

DISHES

Use of all dishes, silver and glasses	10.00
Use of half dishes, silver and glasses	5.00
Glasses, per doz.	.25
Crockery, per doz.	.40
Silver, per doz.	.15

LINEN

Napkins, per doz.	.35
Table cloths, each	.30
Lunch cloths	.15

Our dishes included in any rental, will serve about fifty. One punch bowl and 50 glasses.

Dishes and napkins	16.00

MRS. EARLE S. BARKER, Chairman.

Rental rates circa 1919

Tuesday gathering

The House and Grounds and Tea Room Committees were created to ensure that the clubhouse ran smoothly. In 1913, the Club began to hold informal gatherings on Tuesdays in the summer, which promoted camaraderie during the months when the Club was not in session. The Social Committee worked overtime to keep up with the dramatic increase in membership during these years. The Club increased the limit on the number of members to one thousand in 1913, with a waiting list of nearly one hundred more, and expanded the radius for membership eligibility to within fifteen miles of Evanston.

Repair — Maintain — Expand

Although made of solid brick, the clubhouse nonetheless required maintenance over the years, along with alterations and improvements based on the needs of the members, the community, and the building itself.

With the introduction of monthly luncheons in 1915, the Club changed the flow of the house by opening a third door between the bowling alley and a long corridor and creating an exit between the bowling alley and the street. The Club set aside 15 percent of the rental income to buy new rugs, stage accessories, and a lawn mower, refinish the auditorium floor, repair the roof and gutters, and cover other maintenance expenses.

The Club also bought more property in Evanston. In February 1915, seven hundred women voted to purchase the vacant lot to the north of the clubhouse, 45 feet of frontage on Chicago Avenue, for $3,000. They leveled and seeded the property in summer 1915 and created plans for a garden. When a house at 615 Church Street, just west of the clubhouse, came up for sale in 1918 and the price was reduced by $2,000 to $7,200, the women decided now was the time to buy it and protect the integrity of the clubhouse property. Their rationale, stated in the *Bulletin*, was this: "If we do not buy it now when we can get it, perhaps when we do want it, the owner then would not want to sell—certainly he would not, if he had put a six flat building on it which was bringing him good returns."

In 1919, after a few months without tenants and lacking the funds to renovate the building, the Club decided to join forces with the Girls' League, a social service organization that housed young working women. They used the building to provide housing rent-free to young women doing postwar reconstruction work at Fort Sheridan. The Young Woman's War Relief Auxiliary renovated and furnished the rooms: "Comfortable beds, easy chairs and desk equipment have been provided, color schemes have been successfully carried out in each room in the most artistic and fascinating fashion and charming, unique touches added everywhere." Later, the house provided "rooms for transient girls who may be temporarily stranded in Evanston or temporarily out of work." The April 1921 *Bulletin* reports that, in a period of only six months, the house provided 780 nights of lodging for ninety-two girls. The donation of the house rent-free proved a financial blessing as it further decreased the Club's taxes. In addition to the rent-free use of the building, the Clubwomen pledged $600 to the Girls' League in 1920. The group remained there until 1922, and after that, the Club rented out the house, which was bringing in $75 a month by 1938.

Effectively Consolidating and Collaborating

Considerable overlap began to occur between the various committees—for example, work on local government ordinances was closely tied to social services work—so the Club began to hold joint meetings between various departments and committees. Cooperative committees were formed between the Child and Home and Social Service Departments to ensure that efforts would not be duplicated. In 1915, the number of committees expanded exponentially, demonstrating both the increase in membership and also the desire to run the Club more efficiently. In these years, women affiliated with one department were allowed to join a committee of another department if it suited her interests and abilities. By 1914–1915, Club calendars show that every Tuesday of every month was filled with a department meeting, program, or Club activity, such as sewing for the visiting nurse, House and Grounds, Art and Literature, and the Evanston Welfare Committee,

In November 1913, only eight months after the clubhouse opened, the Club hosted the Nineteenth Annual Conference of the Illinois Federation of Women's Clubs, bringing nine hundred delegates from all over the state to Evanston for a week of networking and collective action. Streamers and pennants welcoming the visiting women adorned houses and residences, along with lights and streamers on Fountain Square and the Woman's Club building and along Church Street and Chicago Avenue. The women worked with the Evanston Commercial Association to provide transportation from train stations and accommodate the delegates in private homes. Luncheons were served in churches all over Evanston at a cost of fifty cents per person. Presentations and entertainment were held in churches and meetings were held in the clubhouse. The Illinois Children's Home and Aid Society, Olympic Club for Boys, Frances Willard House, and businesses all over Evanston invited the delegates to learn more about their activities. The cooperation of the entire community signaled that the Club was well respected and that women's work was taken seriously in this town.

Increasing Philanthropy

*In planning for the coming year do not take up too many
different lines of work unless you are willing to carry the task
undertaken to successful completion. Your husbands, homes,
and families deserve your first consideration. Then come to your
Club Home to enjoy consultations, study, work, entertainment
or sociability. You will find it a hive of industry, a palace of de-
light. The advantages of home and Club are reciprocal.*

—Martha White Hildreth
President, 1915–1917

By the 1910s, the community was providing more support for social services, which allowed for the hiring of social workers and other professionals to perform much of the hands-on work that Club members had previously carried out. However, this work did not completely cease. Group
sewing for the visiting nurse became an annual all-Club event during
1911–1912, and an Institutional Sewing Committee was formed in 1916

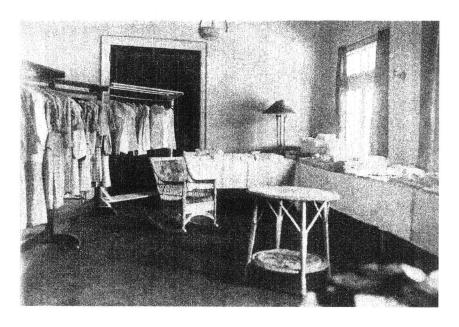

Sewn garments, 1912

to meet monthly to create articles of clothing for organizations all over the Chicago area. This sewing group provided garments for individuals in need while also giving the women a chance to come together to discuss their lives and ideas in an informal setting.

Focusing more and more on philanthropic activities, the Club created a Contributions Committee in 1913–1914, which reviewed the needs of local organizations and disbursed funds to them as donations. In the beginning, the committee devoted 10 percent of the Club's dues for this purpose, but soon began holding fundraisers also. With the establishment of the clubhouse, this committee could more easily hold benefits to raise money. Annual luncheons, dinners, and benefit shows have since become an expected part of Club life, but before the women had a clubhouse, it had not been easy to secure and rent places for these functions. The April 1913 *Bulletin* noted that "the buffet luncheon served by the Social Service Department was a new feature, which, it is hoped, will be repeated next year." By all accounts, this appears to have been the first annual benefit luncheon, which soon evolved to include fashion shows, card games, and performances.

The women also raised money for the Red Cross Tuberculosis Institute through the sale of Christmas seals, which were decorative, collectable stamps. Up to this time, Evanston's tuberculosis nurse had assumed the entire burden of raising funds to fight the deadly virus. As early as 1913, three Clubwomen were appointed to perform a tuberculosis survey in Evanston and make a report to the state federation. In December 1915, Jorinne Turner headed the Red Cross Seals Committee, which raised $708. This was very little compared to later years; the Club raised $5,900 in 1925 and more than $8,000 in 1928 for these "colorful harbingers of Yule cheer." An Evanston Tuberculosis Institute was formed in 1916, hoping to "wipe out this disease in Evanston as far as possible during the present year." The Young Woman's Auxiliary contributed numerous hours to this effort as well, directing the mail campaign and setting up booths in Evanston's businesses and municipal centers, including Marshall Field's and Lord's, Scott Hall on the Northwestern University campus, and the post office.

The Club also continued to raise money to provide positive opportunities for juveniles in the community. After Martha Hildreth, President

ALL FOR HEALTH – HEALTH FOR ALL

1926

MERRY CHRISTMAS

Christmas seals, 1926

from 1915 to 1917, saw the Boy Scouts marching in the 1915 Memorial Day parade, she heard it would be their last appearance due to lack of funds and interest. To help raise funds, she sent out an article titled "The Boy Scouts and My Boy," along with a personalized letter to one thousand addresses. She quickly raised the $10,000 needed to keep the Boy Scouts active in Evanston. By April 1916, Evanston had ten troops, with five more planned.

The Club held classes for women and other groups in need, promoted services that protected women and children, and fought for accessible education and health-care resources. They promoted a local "Baby Week," March 5–11, 1916, an event begun by the General Federation of Women's Clubs and carried out nationally. Mothers obtained clothing, food, and free health care for their children, donated by community members, with the Clubwomen assisting particularly in securing carriages. A Day Nursery Committee was appointed in 1913 to work with the day care run out of the house of Anna Rew Gross, a very early member of the Club. On December 31, 1913, the women held a cafeteria-style luncheon that funded a Christmas party for the mothers and children who were beneficiaries of the Mother's Helping Hand Club and purchased a sewing machine for them that year.

An influx of immigrants into Evanston in the late 1910s led the Club to conduct courses in English and domestic science. The Foreign Neighbors Committee held evening courses at Central School and Stow House, and by September 1915, fifty-five individuals had enrolled. The skills learned were "an important feature of these classes, but undoubtedly the greatest good comes from the developing feeling of friendliness and understanding between these foreign-born women, their children, and ourselves." In 1913, sewing courses had provided employable skills to twenty girls who paid two dollars each for twelve lessons. In an effort to protect women and girls in Evanston, the Club asked the city to hire a policewoman to prevent the abuse of women and girl offenders by male police officers and also funded her training. The Club formed a strong connection with Mary Bartelme, a lawyer and the first woman appointed Cook County Public Guardian, who worked tirelessly with the juvenile court to place girls in foster and protective homes. The Club gave Bartelme a guest ticket in 1912, and members sewed hundreds of garments, up to 150 dresses per year for several years, for Mary's "suitcases," which were filled with clothing and personal goods for every girl who entered the foster care system.

City Watchdogs

The Club took an active interest in ensuring that the city streets were kept clean, sanitary, and beautiful. Helen Dawes, President from 1913 to 1915, called the early years in the clubhouse the "meddlesome" years, as the women's inquiries and inspections saved many lives.

In 1912, the Club's Sanitary Committee wrote a letter to the Evanston Commercial Association demanding that grocers be required to cover exposed food and use tongs to lift food—a request the grocers found startling. Next, the committee divided into groups of two to inspect each of the districts in Evanston and note their concerns with grocers and food carts. The women then appointed an inspector, who was paid $2 a day for twenty-four days to ensure compliance with the new ordinances the Woman's Club had helped established. These ordinances called for the installation of better plumbing, proper cleansing of soda taps, and the raising of fruit and vegetable platforms, among other sanitation improvements. The Club also strongly backed the installation of a water filtration plant, saving many Evanston residents from falling victim to typhoid fever.

In the years leading up to the United States' entry into World War I, the women worked tirelessly in Evanston on "municipal housekeeping," cleaning up the streets as they would their own homes. The Club's Town Improvement Committee, formed in 1916, distributed literature about how to decrease the "fly menace," carried out an Alley Day to inspect the conditions of the alleys, and spearheaded a special garbage service to provide "iron-galvanized" pails for waste pickup two or three times per week. When an inspection revealed inattentive landlords and unsuitable conditions of rental properties, the Club pushed for better regulations and even examined the possibility of public baths. The committee also contributed to Evanston's Plan for Civic Cooperation in February 1916, in which citizens of Evanston registered to take on the task of knowing the ordinances and inspecting and reporting violations.

Many presentations of the Child and Home Department focused on beautification and efficiency in the home, including talks titled "Color as an Exact Science" and "The Housekeeper as Purchasing Agent," as well as seminars on cooking. This increased knowledge of home economics set the stage for conservation efforts carried out during World War I.

Sharing Cultural Experiences with the Community

With an expanding membership the Club increased its connections to groups involved in arts and letters. They began holding joint meetings with the University Guild and sponsored a yearly musicale with the group for the first time in 1916. In 1914, Helen Keller and her teacher, Anne Sullivan Macy, gave a presentation in the clubhouse auditorium. Tickets were one dollar each, and the Club netted $511 in profits, $200 of which went toward the purchase of books for the Evanston Public Library and the rest to a work of art for the clubhouse. Another major event began in 1914 and occurred annually for decades: from March 31 to April 8, 1914, the clubhouse was open from 2 to 6 p.m. for members and friends to view twenty-five paintings on loan from the Thurber, Anders, and O'Brien Gallery and the Artists' Guild. The event was so successful that the women held an even larger exhibit in December 1914. The Special Exhibition of Paintings, Etchings, and Sketches featured the works of artists from the North Shore and brought in an average of $30 dollars a week. The women reprised the event each spring, with brief pauses during the two World Wars. The exhibit grew so large that it took over nearly all rooms of the clubhouse for weeks.

The Art and Literature Department also worked to improve conditions in the community. In cooperation with the Drama Club of Evanston, the women spent several years examining the suitability of the movies shown in the town and the showing of movies on Sundays, going so far as to ask the city to pass an ordinance against inappropriate films. In 1916–1917, the women introduced a "wholesome" movie program at the Strand Theater on Saturdays, but reports indicate that these films were not well attended. They also formed an American Speech Committee, which taught English to immigrants and allowed Club members to study the intricacies of their own language. In the Club's archives, art and literature at first appeared to be a fleeting interest, a side note to the charitable work going on, but its integration into the community had a profound effect.

Suffrage: A Stronger Stance

[I]t is amusing to remember that one of the policies which we sought to establish was that we should attend strictly to our own affairs. We believed that no matter how much we might be interested in such causes as Woman Suffrage, Prohibition, or any question of religion or politics, we should work for them as individual members of their own organizations, but we should not commit our Club as a whole to any of them. In the face of much criticism, we held to this policy until the precedent became firmly established. In my humble opinion, we thereby steered clear of the rocks of dissention on which many an organization has gone to pieces and we are stronger and more useful today as a result of it.

—Helen Dawes
President, 1913–1915

In 1913, the same year that the clubhouse opened, suffrage passed for women in Illinois, which fueled Club affiliations and interest in suffrage. According to the *Bulletin*, attendance grew at both regional and national suffrage conferences, as did donations to suffrage associations including the Illinois Equal Suffrage Association and the North Shore Suffrage Association. The Woman's Club had long provided courses in civics and government, encouraging women to educate themselves and make an impact wherever they could. Catherine Waugh McCulloch, through the Legislative Committee, was instrumental in starting experimental civics classes in 1913 in different parts of town. In the early days, the Club was not very vocal in support of suffrage, but the following passage from the *Bulletin* in March 1913 indicates interest, including a number of charter members:

> On February 17th, Mrs. Ella S. Stewart, ex-President of the Illinois Equal Suffrage Association, was the speaker. Subject, Our New Political Responsibilities. Preceding this meeting a luncheon was served to the members of the department. It was an occasion long to be remembered, for of the ten charter members of the Club who are members of our department, six were present.

World War I: Leading the At Home Response

The Woman's Club's surge in collaboration with other groups could not have come at a more critical time. War was raging in Europe, and the United States was preparing to enter the fight. In February 1917, Martha Hildreth, the outgoing president, sent a letter to every federated club in Illinois, reaching more than 64,000 women. It read: "Prepare to preserve your flag in Peace or defend it in danger. Every woman is saying to herself: 'What can I do?' 'What will I do?'" Two months later, the United States entered the war—on the same day that Catherine Long took office as president of the Woman's Club. "Certainly no President had ever faced any such a new and unexpected situation," she explained. "There were no precedents to guide, no rules of Club conduct to follow. The whole world was in turmoil and the Woman's Club likewise." After her first year

Course in Citizenship for Women Voters

OFFERED BY

THE CIVICS CLASS OF THE WOMAN'S CLUB OF EVANSTON.

I

THURSDAY, JANUARY 15—10 A. M.

The Organization of our City Government—Elective and Appointive Officers.

> Mayor—James R. Smart.
> Director of Public Safety—Walter C. Hedrick.

II

THURSDAY, JANUARY 29—10 A. M.

Some City Activities.

> The Public Works—John H. Moore.
> The Health Department—C. T. Roome, M. D.
> Public Relief—Ruth Bent.

III

THURSDAY, FEBRUARY 12—10 O'clock.

The Sanitary District.

> Commissioner—George W. Paullin.

IV

THURSDAY, FEBRUARY 26—10 A. M.

Taxation—State Board of Equalization.

> Member of State Board—Harry T. Nightingale.

V

THURSDAY, MARCH 12—10 A. M.

The Primaries—Election Methods—Voting.

> City Clerk—John F. Hahn.

VI

THURSDAY, MARCH 26—10 A. M.

Ethics of Citizenship—

> Duty of Becoming Intelligent—
> Using Information.—
> Catherine Waugh McCulloch.

Use will be made of Maps, Charts, Blackboard and other illustrative materials.

The following pamphlets are recommended for aids in study and for reference:

A Hand-book for the Women Voters of Illinois—Alice Greenacre. Price, 25 cents.

The Illinois Women Voters' Hand-book—Mrs. Belle Goodman. Price, 15 cents.

SAVE THIS PROGRAM FOR FUTURE REFERENCE

Civics class syllabus, 1913

in office, Long wrote, "We all felt that we must help and work as we had never worked before. The question at once became what was the work to be done and how were we to do these new, strange tasks which this awful conflict had set us to do?"

Upon the United States' entry into the war, the Woman's Club immediately formed a War Relief Committee, while continuing their work on all other supported reform efforts. The Club was not the only organization in Evanston strongly supporting the war effort, so the women put forth their unique skills where they would be most effective and offered support to activities that could be better carried out by another group.

The Club concentrated its work in three areas: sewing, the purchase of an ambulance, and food conservation. Long asked, "Who does not remember the hive of activity our house became almost immediately?" The Club held Jolly Tar parties for men enlisted in the navy and lectures on the topics of war and international relations and also donated money to organizations such as the Navy Club at Waukegan for the entertainment of servicemen and to the Girls' League's war efforts.

The clubhouse played an integral role in wartime activities. Up until that point, as described by Catherine Long, the clubhouse had been "sacrosanct, a place devoted to hours of profound repose and darkness between the dates of Club or social affairs. A scratch on the mahogany in [the early] days was a tragedy. But now the good old green carpets shrank in astonishment at the pressure of male feet as men in uniform poured into our home to attend our Blighty [an event hosted for British soldiers]." Fee rentals at the clubhouse amounted to $6,640 and went to the Boy Scouts, the Evanston Political Equality League, a demonstration of Public School Music, a meeting about the high cost of living, countless high school dances, and parties for men in uniform. The women also printed a "Roll Call" in each *Bulletin*, acknowledging family members fighting in the war. "What a blessing that we were all so busy!" Long exclaimed. "I do not remember it as a sad time, although over us all hung the shadow of that frightful conflict which might bring disaster and bereavement at any moment."

The Club raised $1,000 to purchase an ambulance through the Chicago chapter of the Red Cross to send to France. The price included "full equipment, transportation, and insurance en route to Europe and nameplate bearing the name of the Woman's Club of Evanston as the donor."

The Club stepped up their sewing activities, producing hundreds of surgical dressings and hospital garments, curtains for the Camp Hospital at Sparta, Wisconsin, bathrobes and pajamas to send to the Great Lakes Training Station, and fifty sweaters for the Red Cross headquarters. After realizing that other organizations were doing much more extensive work, the Club scaled back sewing activities and loaned the clubhouse rent-free to the National Surgical Dressings Committee (under the supervision of Club member May Middleton) and the Young Women's War Relief Unit as a working center. The women continued to sew for the Visiting Nurse Association, Evanston Hospital, Mary Bartelme's girls, Associated Charities, and the Dorcas Home.

Possibly one of the Woman's Club's most successful and famous ventures was the Evanston Community Kitchen, which had its start during World War I. The Club had created a Food Conservation Committee to examine Evanston's efforts and implement programs in this area. In cooperation with seventy-eight other women's groups in the area, the Club collected recipes, surveyed the town to ensure homes and business owners were complying with the United States Food Administration requests, cut back on food served at the clubhouse, taught Evanston families how to grow their own war gardens, and secured pledges to aid in this effort. A conservation lunch with a menu centered on fish was held at the Club, at a cost of $.65 per plate.

A two-day food canning and training session in early 1918 taught conservation skills to twenty-four women and trained them to train others. That summer, the Club held a community canning event in the basement kitchen, which produced 6,649 containers of food. When the influenza epidemic hit Evanston late in the fall of 1918, this concept of a community kitchen continued to serve those too sick to cook for their families. Meals were prepared in the basement of the Woman's Club and then delivered by church volunteers with automobiles. By the end of the epidemic more than 150 families had been served.

Charlotte Perkins Gilman, feminist and noted proponent of the cooperative housekeeping movement, spoke to the Club in February 1919. Her presentation on community cooperation left "the town in the throes of excitement," and prompted the establishment of the Evanston Community Kitchen which opened on May 15, 1919, and ran out of the basement of the Woman's Club, paying rent in the amount of $60 per month. The

Mrs. Rufus Dawes and other members preparing for food delivery, circa 1914

Community Kitchen delivery, circa 1919

kitchen catered to families whose servants had left for jobs in other industries, newlyweds and young mothers, and single businesswomen. Meals were delivered to homes in Aladdin Thermalware containers which kept food hot for hours and were designed specifically for use in the kitchen; the containers were purchased by each family for $30. A weekday dinner for up to four people cost $.85 and $.75 for each additional person; Sunday dinners were $1.00 for regular customers and $1.25 for "casuals"—those who participated only occasionally. Each meal included protein, starch, a vegetable, fruit, and a dessert, and the women served up to 150 homes at a time. When the kitchen became a for-profit business, it had to find a new home as the Club did not support for-profit businesses on its premises. The kitchen moved into a cottage at 1519 Davis Street in March 1920 and soon discontinued delivery service. In 1925 the kitchen moved to 600 Davis Street, where it remained a carryout food service, cafeteria, and bakery until 1951.

Club Business as Usual

Even while working hard for the war effort, the Club realized that other needs remained pressing. When the United States entered the war, then President Catherine Long warned:

> Shall our armies return to find that what they left
> behind has been safe guarded by us who have stayed,
> or shall they find our cherished institutions tottering,
> our hard won victories in reform lost, our ideals of right
> living abandoned, our future citizenship imperiled, our
> womanhood and childhood depleted by overwork and low
> standards of living? . . . In the period of reconstruction
> after the war is over may our task be the lighter because of
> the effort we shall make now to keep life normal, serene
> and beautiful and to preserve our own organization strong,
> harmonious and superlatively useful.

And so the women continued other activities not directly related to the war effort. They gave Club membership tickets to Evanston teachers, donated $50 to the safety island for pedestrians in Fountain Square and $30 for wastebaskets to be placed around Evanston, supported a policewoman in completing a training course, and studied the possibility of declaring an official flower for Evanston, leaving the final decision between a nasturtium, zinnia, or marigold to schoolchildren. They worked with the Butcher's and Grocer's Committee, a local group, to secure a half holiday each week for grocery clerks, continued their crusade to improve the quality of available entertainment by showing movies on Sunday, and held two benefit card parties—one for the Mary Bartelme Homes and another for the Young Woman's War Relief Unit. The Club suspended the annual art exhibit during this period but held other exhibits, including one on war posters that featured artists from different parts of the country. The Art and Literature Department decided to hold an annual play during the war, which "made an agreeable change from lectures, and would now be a relief from having our nerves shattered by guesses upon the trend of world politics." Indeed, without a gathering space in the center of town where members could come together to lift each other up during this difficult time, the work of the Woman's Club—and many other social services and war-related organizations—would have crumbled. The construction of the clubhouse could not have come at a more opportune time.

While the war raged on, the Club invited former president William Howard Taft to come to Evanston to speak in Patten Gymnasium on the topic of universal military training, making $1,763 from ticket sales. A quarantine during the influenza epidemic delayed his speech. The Club rescheduled his appearance for November 11, 1918, a date that coincidentally marked the end of World War I and became known as Armistice Day or Veteran's Day.

Repairing House, Home, and Soul

A great organization like ours is too important an asset to society to be endangered by anything so transient as all wars must

be, and the value of the woman trained in organizations has
been proved over and over again in the last two years. . . . We
have never been more fit for service than we are today.

—Catherine Long
President, 1917–1919

The war left the Club exhausted and its beautiful new clubhouse looking years older than its actual six. "Now the war was over," reflected
Stanwood at the Club's fortieth anniversary, "all the glow of enthusiastic
patriotism that had warmed the whole country had faded. . . . The Woman's Club faced its fourth decade with deflated spirit. The interior of its
beautiful Clubhouse had been made shabby by wartime activities which
had been hospitably housed, and regular Club work had been lessened
by the pressure of war service." The Club had never faced anything as
devastating as World War I, but its deflated spirit did not last long, and
the women soon were back at work and responding to the needs of the
postwar world.

Beginning in October 1918, general Club days became "Open Forum"
days, with the floor opened to all members to discuss any topic. According to the *Bulletin*, these were "one of the most popular afternoons of the
month. Its object was to encourage expression of everyone's thoughts and
to enable a member to state and sustain an opposing view, in other words
to say what she had to say in meeting and not on the way home." The
Club aided Evanston's new Thrift House, which provided secondhand
wares to individuals in need at a modest price with the proceeds split
among a number of local charities. Women could also bring in handmade items and baked goods to sell, receiving 10 percent of the profit to
cover expenses. Following the war, in 1920, the Thrift House moved to a
larger space at 719 Main Street in order to accommodate an increase in
the number of customers. All of the saleswomen, which included many
Woman's Club members, were volunteers, and their charity of choice
would receive proceeds based on the amount of time each woman worked.

Another postwar undertaking was Library Day, which was first held at
the clubhouse on March 18, 1919. The women who attended heard a talk,
"Public Libraries in Their Relations to Public Education and the Problems of Americanization," and saw exhibits on how to use the library to
"gain a more extensive education through [one's] own initiative." Library

Days raised money for the Library Emergency Fund in 1921. In 1923, the clubhouse opened its doors for the Evanston Public Library's fiftieth anniversary celebration. Ida Faye Wright, librarian and women's historian, wrote in a letter to Mrs. William G. Alexander, November 3, 1923:

> The opening of your building for the evening program
> and reception, thereby making possible a "progressive
> party" was one of the loveliest examples of community
> neighborliness of which we know. The Librarians from
> many parts of the state who attended the celebration
> all marveled at the very unusual cooperation which the
> Woman's Club of Evanston extends to the Public Library.
> Not only do we appreciate all that the Club did toward
> making festive the golden jubilee celebration, but we are
> constantly mindful of the debt which we owe the Club for
> the many acts of neighborly service which it bestows upon
> the Library.

Young Women Welcomed

Looking for ways to increase its "woman power" after the war, the Club created the Young Woman's Auxiliary. Many young women in Evanston had worked for the war effort, obtained jobs when the men were away fighting, and held college degrees. The Woman's Club realized that these talented young women needed a postwar outlet and that they could be a strong force for good in the community. Catherine Long, Laura Vickers, and Adele Hall sent out invitations to "suggested candidates" that read: "A Junior Auxiliary of the Woman's Club of Evanston is contemplated. An equipment of over 25 years' growth, amidst unusual surroundings, is offered to those who desire to unite for artistic, dramatic, social, literary and philanthropic purposes." The Club accepted 121 charter members between the ages of eighteen and twenty-eight. In the first year, initiation fees were $3 and annual fees were $5, with the proceeds going to the Woman's Club for use of their building. The Auxiliary held its first official meeting on April 26, 1919, with membership restricted to two hundred in the first year, only to be raised to three hundred in 1923 with the age range increased to thirty-two. Agnes Betts McCulloch, daughter-in-law of Catherine McCulloch, served as the Auxiliary's first president. Many daughters and nieces of former and current Club members became Auxiliary members.

Agnes Betts McCullough,
First President of the Young
Woman's Auxiliary, 1919

The *Evanston News-Index* expressed its approval of the Auxiliary: "The future holds for women lines of activity, opportunities for service unthought of today except by those few who have their eyes set upon the things that are to be. Women are just beginning to sense the new freedom that is theirs, just beginning to feel the power that they are inheriting from the work of those pioneers who have secured their emancipation." The Auxiliary's programs reflected its membership; for example, a newlyweds' class to teach "young married couples . . . how to make a home. The first lesson Saturday will be on serving meals." In its recognition of the needs and potential of this next generation of women, the Auxiliary members were pioneers in the discussion of how to balance family, home, and work—a topic that continues to challenge women today.

The Auxiliary experienced some growing pains at first. Forgetting that personal connections, bonds, and friendships are so important to forming the solid foundation of any successful organization, the founders had failed to provide the "personal touch" that new members wanted: "A printed card will not do it. That cup of tea will be drunk alone whether she puts a cross after the things that interest her or not," read a letter from member Lavinia Harris to Adele Hall, March 1, 1921. Realizing their mistake, the Auxiliary expanded their efforts to reach out to new regular members of the Club and to married women who had recently moved to Evanston. Back in those days Evanston wasn't nearly as large as it is today, so news of new residents traveled quickly. It was typically frowned upon for wealthier women with husbands to work, so they were prime targets for membership in a philanthropic organization.

In these first years, the Auxiliary immediately began raising money for local organizations. In one of its earliest acts of service, the Auxiliary took charge of the Thrift House's luncheon in late 1919. Other activities are documented by letters from charitable organizations that are pasted into early scrapbooks in the Club's archive, noting contributions to child welfare groups, the Cook County Juvenile Court, sewing for the Visiting Nurse Association, and eradicating child labor (the Auxiliary led a 1919 membership campaign in Evanston for the National Child Labor Committee). A letter from Mary Bartelme acknowledges $50 received from the Auxiliary to purchase shoes for girls in the foster system. "I held some of the money back until last week when several of our girls were graduating from the Eighth Grade," Bartelme wrote, "a very great event in their lives, and I wish you could have seen one little girl who came all the way downtown from 48th Street to show me her shoes, her flowers and class colors. I am sure you would have felt it worthwhile to have paid $50.00 for the one pair of shoes could you have seen the joy and earnestness of this little girl of fifteen who had had so little in life."

The Auxiliary celebrated its tenth anniversary on April 6, 1929, with a "pretty ceremony . . . [and] the cutting of the birthday cake, which stood in the center of the dining room, twined with smilax and flowers and topped with a white horseshoe." In addition to philanthropy and community service, the Auxiliary held educational programs on travel, world affairs, civic responsibilities, and the arts; numerous dances, balls, and teas; and provided self-improvement activities and outlets for its members, such as a Drama Club and Glee Club.

Rethinking Community Impact

As the Progressive Era in the United States wound down, many social service agencies were formed and received funding from government sources. The Woman's Club constantly reexamined these new services, served on boards of directors and advisory councils, and endeavored to fill in whatever gaps remained. Drawing once again on their roles as wives and mothers, the women provided the personal touch that accelerated the physical and emotional healing process.

The women sent gifts to agencies caring for those in need — toys, books, and jars of jelly to a children's hospital, for example — and provided automobile rides to the sick and elderly. The Club's County Welfare Committee donated fruit, bedroom slippers, and Christmas decorations to the Cook County Hospital in 1921–1922. These hand-delivered, often hand-made, goods provided a much-needed boost and increased morale among recipients, which was especially important after the war.

In the decades following the war, the women took a great interest in international relations. In December 1921, President Edith Ennis appointed a committee to work for "World Friendship and World Peace." After sending letters to all potentially interested women's groups in Evanston, an all-Evanston International Relations Committee was created, made up of nineteen different organizations. The Woman's Club committee was selected to serve as the executive directors. The first meeting on May 14, 1925, featured several women speaking on "What Organized Women Can Do to Avert War." The committee taught children about world citizenship and reached out to international students at Northwestern. The group set plans in place to send relief to Russia and heard talks on Tokyo, Czechoslovakia, and the cause and cure for war. In July 1925, the organization became one of the sponsors of a series of lectures called the Evanston School of Foreign Affairs (later World Affairs). This international focus continued through the interwar period and the Second World War. In the *Fortieth Anniversary* booklet, in 1929, Long wrote: "I hope and have faith to believe that we shall never have to go through another war. If the Great War taught us anything at all, it was that disputes can never be settled that way among nations any more than they can among individuals. . . . My hope for my beloved club is that when love, justice and peace shall abide upon and rule the earth, it shall have had its part in bringing about this millennium."

The Inter-racial Relations Committee, created in 1921–1922, sought to build bridges between groups of people in Evanston. An influx of African Americans had moved to the Chicago area before, during, and after the war. To address the needs of this new community group, the committee financially supported the North Shore Community House, a boarding house for African American women on the corner of Garrett and Ridge that was managed by the Iroquois League, an African American women's organization. In addition, the Club provided the financial backing for a "colored day nursery" for children of working women.

The Club's City Affairs Committee worked to eliminate the "frequent duplication of effort [by various organizations] with its consequent waste — waste which can be ill-afforded when there is so much to be done." The committee invited social service and welfare agencies to the clubhouse for a Hospitality Day to discuss their activities and ensure cooperation. Of the seventeen groups invited, sixteen agreed to participate. Later called the Evanston Social Service Exchange, on December 6, 1928, the women hosted the following organizations:

Kiwanis Club

Optimist Club

Rotary Club

Elks Club

Mothers Clubs

Churches

American Legion Hospital Association

Police Department Association of Charities

Junior League Welfare Associations

City hall

Schools

Although Illinois suffrage passed in 1913, national suffrage would not be passed until 1920. During these interim years, the Club sent delegates to conferences on the topic and became involved in organizations such as the North Shore Suffrage Institute. The Club provided space free of rent to the Evanston Political Equality League for their Institute of Citizenship in 1920, continued their legislative committee to learn about bills, and sent out letters regarding candidates and elections. A letter regarding an election for circuit court judges in 1921 notes: "It has always been the unwritten policy of the Woman's Club of Evanston to take no part in politics," but the letter went on to encourage women to vote nonpartisan due to the heavy responsibility of this office. Jeannette Rankin, the first congresswoman in the United States, elected in 1916, visited the Woman's Club in 1921 and spoke on "Women as Voting Constituents."

The League of Women Voters was created nationally upon the achievement of suffrage, with the nonpartisan mission to ensure women's needs were met and "to educate the electorate, [and] insure a standardization of beneficial laws concerning women and children." The Woman's Club collaborated with this group and held a joint meeting in 1926. Many hoped that the league would become irrelevant as the electorate would soon recognize the importance of meeting the needs of women and children. This was not to be, and the league continues to address the needs of women voters and their families in Evanston and throughout the nation.

Reorganizing the Organization

As the Club faced a growing membership, diversifying interests, and more partnerships with other organizations, it sought to better organize, record, and streamline its activities. An Archives Committee was started in 1916–1917 to preserve the Club's memory and materials. The first full-time secretary, Laura Knaggs, was hired in 1920, and the Club has since depended heavily on the spectacular work of its paid employees. This first hiring signaled the Club's desire to become truly modern by engaging in the more streamlined and efficient business practices that had been developed during the Industrial Revolution. A telephone was installed in the president's home to facilitate communications in 1919, and in 1920 an addressograph and new filing cabinets were added to the clubhouse furnishings, making the Club "realize the business side of our organization which is constantly growing." In 1922, the Club purchased a typewriter and mimeograph. All of these changes paid off: in February 1925, Lydia Betts reported that she was able to reduce the Club's taxes from $2,474 to $1,278 by demonstrating the community work and charitable donations of the Club. To ensure transparency, the Club used an outside professional accountant to audit the treasurer's report each year.

During the 1920s, the *Bulletin* became a substantial publication, a magazine of some fifty pages with photographs and an index, operating in the black. The advertising committee started selling more and more ads, although not without comment from the members: "there was wailing over having to stop in the middle of an article and 'turn to page 50.' There were remarks suggesting that the reading matter was not sufficiently interesting to hunt the conclusion, but the club members soon became interested in seeing whose picture had been printed." Reinforcing their new professionalism, the Woman's Club became affiliated with the newly created Evanston Business and Professional Women's Club.

The Club also worked tirelessly to return the clubhouse to its original prewar state. Its use during the war, though beneficial, had taken a toll on the floors, windows, and furniture. Starting in 1920–1921, the Club set aside 35 percent of its income for ongoing clubhouse maintenance, which would further safeguard the house from continued wear and tear. The clubhouse was being heavily used: by 1923–1924, the Club had reached its limit of 1,000 members, with an additional 62 nonresident members and 264 auxiliary members, for a total of 1,326 members, with 319 names on the waiting list. During this year, the Club held 964 activities and rented out the clubhouse for 447 events; all told 104,552 individuals walked through its doors. To offset the cost of maintenance the Club raised rental rates by 25 percent (with special rates for students), eliminated free rentals, and raised membership dues.

The new rules, increases in dues, and meticulous recordkeeping paid off: by 1925, the treasurer's report shows no mortgage bond payments on the Club's properties. It seems that the Club paid it off a little too quickly for the bank's tastes, however: "We exerted ourselves to pay [the mortgage] off as speedily as possible and were greatly surprised to get word from the Bank that we were paying it off too fast," noted Mrs. Helen B. Dawes. "That was when many of us learned for the first time that a mortgage sometimes represents a respectable investment. We substituted more reasonable payments and invested our surplus income in the lot adjoining our property on the north. Even in quarters that seemed to us truly palatial, we already foresaw the time when we should need room for expansion." While this was an occasion to celebrate, the Club also had reason to mourn. They had learned, through a telegram from her husband, that founder Elizabeth Boynton Harbert had died in Pasadena, California, on January 19, 1925.

Changing with the Times

The activities of the average housewife are diversified. With the church, school, home, social and civic interests her days are full. Her own pursuit of the necessary daily routine duties and pleasure, augmented by the supervision of her self-sufficient modern family make of our present-day Clubwoman and home-maker a very versatile being.

—Margaretha Helm
Chair of the Home Department, 1923–1924

Many social services had fallen by the wayside during wartime only to be picked up again by newly organized and well-supported community agencies, many of which had roots in the efforts of the Woman's Club. For example, in 1920 child welfare work—long a concern of the Woman's Club—finally became a regular part of the activities of Evanston's Health Department; a resolution on this is mentioned in the Executive Committee's minutes for November 17, 1919. The Club needed to find ways to fit into this changing landscape. They did so by filling in the gaps and providing personal care, touring facilities and serving on boards of directors, and creating new services.

The changing landscape in social service provision led the Club to become more social in the late 1920s and continuing through the 1930s without abandoning its commitment to service and philanthropy. They continued giving 10 percent of their dues to charity and raised money for specific endeavors through programs. An increase in social events during this period promoted the longevity of the Club by providing a way for the women to connect, form relationships, and lift their morale in a time of extreme domestic trouble just ahead—the Great Depression.

The women, however, did not just sit around and talk. They became more interested in art and literature at this time—as producers as well as consumers—by winning poetry and scrapbook awards, creating book reviews, and taking writing courses.

The Club organized a popular poetry class in 1927, and on October 18, 1927, the Fine Arts Department held a book fair. Even though opinion was mixed—one member told the book class that they should be discussing affairs of the home and family rather than reading "those silly books"—the class became so popular that it had to be moved from a lecture room to the ballroom. Famous guests came through the clubhouse, including poet Carl Sandburg in 1928; the guestbook is a treasure trove and testimony to the clout that the Club held with artists, writers, and musicians. The Club also valued work from those who were not so famous, holding an exhibit of arts and crafts from Evanston shops and

Needlework Committee, 1925

Club members in January 1929 and continuing the popular annual art exhibit. With the increase in events and rentals, the Club needed more staff to manage its affairs; by 1928–1929, nearly $10,000 was spent annually on employee salaries.

The Club continued its work on social services, home economics, and education. In 1925, the Needlework Committee bought six electric sewing machines and produced 571 articles of clothing and goods in 1928–1929. The Committee on Friendly Cooperation with Service Men purchased one thousand wool sweaters for veterans in need and produced entertainment and decorations for the Red Cross Recreational Hall and the Naval Hospital, boosting the morale of former soldiers and sailors. The Home and Education Department heard talks on home economics and decor, including "The Business Side of Homemaking," and continued their connection with the Parent-Teacher Association. The department formed a Child Labor Committee when stricter child labor laws were posed in 1926 and pledged to educate the public about this dangerous practice and to monitor school attendance in Evanston. The Social Service Department held a Current Events course for the Club under the leadership of May Wood Simons and toured institutions around Chicago, including the Cook County Jail and the Institute for Juvenile Research. The women also participated in smaller acts of charity around the state, including sending 150 books to Murphysboro, Illinois, which was ravaged by a deadly tornado in 1925, and contributing money to the Boy Scouts so that they could purchase land for Camp Wabaningo.

Celebrating Forty Years

It has been said— "Our grand business undoubtedly is not to see what lies simply at a distance, but to do what lies clearly at hand." . . . We do not know where the future will carry us but we do know, that without the vision of continued service to a growing community our Club life must perish. "Our doubts are traitors and make us lose the good we oft might win by fearing to attempt."

—Beulah Spofford
President, 1927–1929

By the fortieth anniversary, celebrated on March 26, 1929, the Club had raised its membership limit to 1,200, not counting nonresident members; in all, 1,328 women were considered members of the Club, with 300 more on the waiting list. In one month in 1929, the Club carried out seventy-one activities with 12,432 participants. They gave luncheons to welcome new members and matched some newcomers with established members. In 1927, the president urged the Building Committee to explore expanding the clubhouse. That year, the ventilating system was improved, and the Club bought new ovens and a new piano. In 1929, the partition between the parlor and tearoom had been removed to enlarge the gathering space. In 1928–1929, the Club took its first thorough inventory of everything in the house for insurance purposes; the paintings alone were valued at about $15,000. Like the bubbling economy leading up to the Depression, the Club was ever expanding and reaching new heights that were likely never thought possible when the women first gathered to meet at Harbert's house on that cold winter evening in March 1889.

The women celebrated their fortieth anniversary at the clubhouse with great fanfare. A conversation between charter and early members discussing the founding years of the Club was recreated on stage, with Harbert's niece playing the part of her aunt while members of the Club's Young Women's Auxiliary played supporting roles. No guests were permitted due to lack of space; only Club members, Auxiliary members, and those on the waiting list were invited to the auditorium to view the production, which started promptly at two o'clock and lasted two hours, followed by a reception for charter members. Over these forty years, the role of women in society had changed drastically with the increased availability of education, the passage of suffrage, and women's participation in the Great War. The role of the Club itself would change in the coming decades, with the coming of the Great Depression and yet another world war, but there was no doubt the members would continue to meet the needs of the community.

"When the last Club certificate's issued
And the last dollar's honestly earned,
When the Club's last debt has been cancelled
And the bonds are redeemed and burned
We shall rest; and faith we shall need it
Lie down for an aeon or two
Till some other good leader of women
Shall put us to work anew".

Author unknown.
From 40th Anniversary Booklet

40th Anniversary of the Woman's Club of Evanston, 1929.
Former presidents (seated L-R): Mrs. Charles E. Clifton, Mrs. Robert Berry Ennis,
Mrs. Charles H. Betts, Mrs. Rufus C. Dawes, Mrs. Charles W. Spofford,
Mrs. Ulysses S. Grant, Mrs. Towner K. Webster, Mrs. William G. Alexander,
Mrs. George W. Kaufmann, and Mrs. John Harper Long.

CHAPTER THREE

Endurance: 1930s through the 1950s

It has been a pleasant road we have traveled together. As to scene, direction, and company, it would be in any circumstances the road of my choice. If Evanston be "a state of mind," what a delightful state of mind in which to be!

—Rosalie Elliot
President, 1929–1931

The Roaring Twenties brought a sense of happiness and comfort to the Woman's Club of Evanston. The economy continued to thrive, and so did the Club. Membership was at an all-time high with a 1,200-person limit and hundreds more on the waiting list, the properties were paid off, members were actively learning and creating, and social services were streamlined and carried out with ease. Four decades in the community had taught the Woman's Club how to organize, manage, and be efficient and creative at the same time, and the members felt ready to meet any challenge. Then, only seven months after that festive fortieth anniversary celebration, the stock market crashed in October 1929, plunging the country into the Great Depression.

The Great Depression

Though at times we have looked into the Valley of Depression, we have never been down-hearted, but with even step, ever courageous, ever joyous, we have wended our way upward.

—Alice Scott
President, 1931–1933

Tea Room

Like the rest of the nation, the Club and its members were hit hard by the Great Depression. Membership numbers decreased slightly, and the women began the 1933 Club year in debt due to a nationwide bank moratorium. But, as President Lydia Burr (1933–1935) pointed out, the Club survived when many others did not in part because they had a clubhouse and other properties that were completely paid off.

During 1932–1933, the board took measures to reduce financial hardship on new members. To address dwindling membership, the Club waived the initiation fee for several months—later reinstating it at a reduced rate of $15—and allowed members to pay dues in two, three, or four installments. To expand the pool of potential members, in 1937, the women voted to open membership to women within a 45-mile radius of the Club, an action that some women felt would diminish the Club's prestige. Along with the fee reductions, employee salaries were reduced by 10 percent in March 1933. Even with these reductions in fees and luncheon prices, members still questioned where the money was going. Luncheons were served by the Club on a regular basis, and costs were reduced, first to 50 cents and then to 35 cents. A supper/bridge party in 1932 cost only $1.25 to attend. The Club could not reduce its many contributions to the community, as this allotment of funds was stipulated in its bylaws and because the women knew that the community depended on them. The board also decided it could not reduce the percentage of dues used to maintain the clubhouse because the Club depended on income from rentals; and they were not willing to further reduce dues because members were getting the most for their money.

The Club reduced costs in other ways. Logs were no longer burned in the fireplace on Tuesdays and Fridays to conserve resources. Paper napkins and tablecloths could be used for Club luncheons over cloth ones to reduce laundry costs, but "these seemed not in great favor with the Board. It was suggested that lighter lunches be served." Table linens were a symbol of status and luxury for the Club in a time of instability. If they could not pursue projects requiring big expenditures, they wanted to hold onto the little touches to maintain some sense of normalcy.

The board reduced budgets for departments, committees, and Club activities up to 50 percent, partly in response to reduced membership. However, with the temporary waiver and later reduction of the initiation fee, the Club filled their membership within three months of the start of the 1932 Club year and a "symbol of prosperity and peace" was once again created: the waiting list. With this increased income from new members, the Club was able to make clubhouse improvements, including installing stage lighting in the auditorium, which in turn increased income from rentals. As a result, the women put $2,000 into their sinking fund (money set aside for repaying debt and managing depreciation of their properties, created in 1925), double what they had set aside the year before. Although the Club endured its share of hardships, it fared better than many other Clubs due to the careful planning of past presidents and counselors. The women who kept the Club alive during the trying time of the Great Depression are to be commended.

Still Committed to the Community

To me, social service implies an extension of our Club into the very life of our city—to provide guidance, cheer, and comfort, not only to ourselves, but to those less fortunate. May it ever be the goal towards which this department aims.

—Jean Reynolds
Social Services Chair, 1936–1937

Despite financial hardships, the women donated an extraordinary amount of money, goods, and hours of service to meet community needs. Many social service agencies were now funded by government sources; others functioned independently. As a result, the Club's role changed: rather than having the Woman's Club help to *start* them, these organization needed help to *continue and grow.* The Club contributed 10 percent of its income to a variety of charities around Evanston, donating an impressive sum of $2,000 to $3,000 each year based on dues alone during the Depression. But social services foundered throughout the decade. An article in the *Evanston Index* in 1935 noted that "the Infant Welfare Association continues as a private agency, the work abandoned by the frugal city a few years ago." Such financial hardship motivated the Club to raise money in any way possible for emergency needs of civic and social service not normally included in the Club's annual 10 percent contribution.

During the Depression, the Woman's Club collected money and goods by placing orange barrels and milk bottles around Evanston. The Orange Barrels drive, initially headed by the Social Services Department, became an all-Club effort. Food items were collected in the barrels, and local theaters gave movie admission in exchange for goods. In 1931, Evanston residents donated $1,600 worth of food. On November 26, 1932, thirteen barrels of food were collected at a single motion picture benefit at the Valencia Theater. The women noted that 350 cans of tomatoes were among the donations, and that next time, the emphasis should be placed on coffee. Milk bottles served as a depository for spare change when citizens were out shopping. The bottles generated $150 in 1931 and $250 in 1936. These donations were used by the Holiday Bureau, which had been started by the Club and taken over by the city of Evanston in 1934, to create baskets of food and other goods for those in need at Thanksgiving

Orange Barrel Program,
1931

Milk bottle for change collection,
1931–36

and Christmas. In 1932, Club members packed 370 baskets for Thanksgiving and 800 for Christmas.

Annual card party benefits were another successful fundraising tool during this decade. These parties were a fun way to raise money for various organizations. In 1935, the card party benefit raised $450 for the Community Chest, Family Welfare Association, and the Unemployed Youth Movement, an amount that the department chair considered substantial "under these conditions." In 1936 the Club again held a benefit bridge party to raise funds. The Club also gave Christmas parties for the Park Ridge School for Girls and for the kindergarten at the Northwestern University Settlement.

The women continued their interest in physical health, giving $215 dollars in 1930 to have a printing plate made for birth registration certificates through the Department of Health in Evanston. They sponsored a Civic Health Exhibit in Evanston during the early 1930s, which in 1933 brought in thirty-five organizations and more than three thousand visitors. The Christmas seals drive to fight tuberculosis, begun in 1915, continued, and the donations, though decreasing during the Depression, still reached thousands of dollars per year—$8,307.41 in 1930 alone. The Young Woman's Auxiliary took an especially prominent role in helping with the Christmas seals campaign in this decade and beyond, fully sponsoring the drive in 1937 with the Club serving as an advisory board. In 1938, the Auxiliary opened seven thousand donation letters, distributed supplies of posters and printed materials to schools, and led the sale of "bangle pins," wearable emblems representing the fight against tuberculosis. These pins were sold to schoolchildren for one penny to encourage their participation.

The women also stayed informed on current topics. International presentations abounded on Russia, North Africa, Germany, Mexico, and London. Other presentations focused on a variety of topics, including bills regarding maternal and infant health, motion pictures, married women's right to work and serve on jury duty, the state Prohibition law, and disarmament, as well as reports on prisons and settlement houses. The women visited institutions in Chicago and Evanston, including Hull House, the lower North Relief Station, the Criminal Court, and Bridewell Prison (now Cook County Correctional Facility). Mrs. Wilson V. Little, chair of the Trips to Institutions Committee maintained that "by visiting these institutions we have gained a more sympathetic and intelligent understanding of some of the problems that they are trying to solve, thus enabling us to make a fairer appraisal of the work they are carrying on." In 1931, the women took an interest in the Chicago Plant, Flower, and Fruit Guild, which sent goods to city institutions that needed a boost in morale and aesthetics.

In addition to handmade goods such as layettes and knitted items made by the Welfare Sewing Committee, the women distributed thousands of birthday cards, playing cards, magazines, paperweights, and yarn to the Veteran's Hospital in Chicago and other institutions. Ex-servicemen at the Occupational Therapy Hospital also participated in arts and crafts, creating items which were then sold in exhibits at the clubhouse, netting $112.60 for the veterans in 1931. The Committee on Friendly Cooperation with Ex-Service Men was very active during this decade, throwing holiday parties, donating goods such as books, magazines, games, clothing, candy, and cigarettes, and baking cakes and cookies. The women recognized that the needs of soldiers did not stop with the war.

An Explosion of Creativity

This Club, the third largest in the United States, where practically all members are college graduates, is becoming almost a graduate school for creative writers, French, speech, and drama students, and rightly so. We are no longer content to listen exclusively, but wish to contribute somehow in a creative way toward the enjoyment of life.

— Ruth Lawson
Fine Arts Chair, 1938–1939

No department saw as much growth and activity as the Art and Literature Department. In the late 1920s, the women had become not only consumers, but also producers of their own works, and they won several awards, especially in the area of poetry. The social unrest of the 1930s stimulated creativity and allowed for greater experimentation and expression in art and literature, while also providing a diversion from the difficulties of the Depression. "The modern woman needs to do something with her hands as a relaxation from strenuous life," said Lydia Burr in an *Evanston Index* article about Clubwomen and quilting. While on the surface it may appear self-serving or wasteful to pursue arts and crafts in a time of such need in the country, these activities brought happiness to individuals and stability and purpose to organizations impacted by the Depression. At the Woman's Club of Evanston, numerous writers spoke about their work, including poet Robert Frost, who spoke in 1932 at the annual joint meeting with the University Guild.

After a poetry class was established at the Club in the 1920s, the women began winning awards in regional and state contests. During 1935–1936, Club members took home six of the eight possible awards in the poetry and short story contest held by the 10th District of the Illinois Federation of Women's Clubs. Anna Scott, who had a doctorate degree in literature and was a children's book author, won first place in the 10th District poetry contest in 1933–1934 with the following poem:

The Peasant Maid in "The Song of the Lark"

A lark I cannot see has winged his flight
From clover fields fresh bathed with dew
To clouds, those blessed islands of blue
Where sits enthroned the choir of angels white.

The clouds are gold inside for I can see
Their shining edges curling rim on rim,
And I can all but hear the angel's hymn
Tuned with the lark's in joyous harmony.

All through my day of toil until my eyes
Shut out the world from me, my heart will sing
The sky-lark's song; his heaven-ward horning wing
Will blow me golden dreams of Paradise.

The Club kept elaborate scrapbooks documenting the members' activities and publicity nearly every year beginning in 1922. These evolved over the course of a decade to include newspaper clippings, letters, ribbons, photographs, copies of the Club's yearbook and each *Bulletin* from that year, and much more. The women also took classes in creative writing, public speaking, music, and book reviews, held dramatic readings and put on plays, and started a Club chorus in 1939. The annual art exhibits continued, and the Club began awarding prizes to the participants in 1931. In 1934, the Club held monthly art exhibits open to the public. The annual exhibit in 1935 featured 296 pieces from 165 artists. The General Federation of Women's Clubs at this time sponsored a Penny Art Fund in which each member donated one penny to a national fund, which was used to purchase a work of art for clubs that promoted art in their community. Participation in the fund by the Woman's Club of Evanston was one hundred percent in 1935.

Beauty In, Out, and Around

In these times of confusion and crisis, when pressure from so many sides has disturbed the equilibrium of mind and soul, we have endeavored to bring into our Club the stabilizing influence of Beauty. For us it has been a happy and grateful task.

—Flora Dodson Skipp
Art Committee Chair, 1932–1933

Art Show, circa 1936

Art Show

The women also sought to bring beauty to Evanston and the country. The Garden Committee cared for the clubhouse grounds, and the Club developed strong ties with the Garden Club of Evanston. On April 1, 1930, the Club held its first annual flower show in the auditorium under the direction of Betty Shutterly. The next year, the Club had six exhibits in the annual flower show of the Illinois Federation of Women's Clubs, held at the Sherman Hotel, and they took home an honorable mention for their luncheon table. The Club welcomed 485 participants to a three-day garden institute in 1937, an event that was continued in subsequent years. The Floral Committee provided decor for the Club's many luncheons and parties.

At the end of the 1920s, women's clubs all over the nation took up the conservation movement, and the Woman's Club followed suit. The Club called for the 1935–1936 duck and geese hunting season to be closed, as drought and overhunting were diminishing species' numbers. The Club wrote a letter to Governor Horner in May 1935 promoting a board-approved resolution to endorse the Protection of Wild Flowers and Beauty Spots in Illinois and sought to protect elm trees from destruction in the state. These acts of conservation were no doubt pursued in response to Franklin Delano Roosevelt's New Deal, the devastation of the Dust Bowl, and knowledge gained during conservation efforts made in wartime. They also represented attempts at the reconstruction and preservation of the order of society; if society was experiencing economic unrest, perhaps the natural world could be saved.

Making Our Work Fun

The ownership of a Clubhouse such as ours is a luxury. But, like the ownership of a home, it is worth the anxiety and effort sometimes necessary to maintain it. It is not merely a shelter. Rather—a symbol of the self-sacrifice, unity of purpose and ideals upon which it has been built, and of the close companionship through joys and sorrows which have been experienced within its walls. A loyal and devoted member of a Club or a home is willing to make the extra effort to sustain it in its time of need.

—Lydia Burr
President, 1932–1934

Despite the Club's financial hardships during the Great Depression, income rose with increased membership. The Club was able to reinvest this money in clubhouse improvements and another property. A public address system was installed in the clubhouse in 1934 to better communicate with the growing number of members and visitors who came through its doors. That year, the Club began to hold Open House Fridays, which gave departments an opportunity to mingle with one another and allowed members to pursue new interests and enjoy various programs.

The Club continued to promote openness to individuals of all backgrounds. In 1933, their secretary, Laura Knaggs, appeared before the board to confess what she thought was a mistake. After booking singer Mabel Roberts Walker to perform at the Club, she discovered that the performer was African American and she didn't know what to do. Lydia Burr, president at the time, replied, "There is no reason why the reservation should not stand."

This surge of activity inspired the women to make the clubhouse more social as well. During 1936–1937, the Club spent $2,742 (with another $1,856 for furnishings) to transform the south porch into a member's lounge, adding to the "comfort of the members as well as to the social possibilities of the Clubhouse." During the summer of 1938, the Club remodeled the upper porch off the ballroom and made it fit for winter parties at a cost of $1,758. Even in the midst of the Depression, the Club was able to purchase tables, linen, silver, and china to make up complete dinner service for five hundred. While these expenditures may seem lavish in the face of the economic crisis, the social events held the women together at a time when the Club was redefining its role in the community. Evening parties, luncheons, plays, presentations, and classes provided an escape from hardships and attracted more members and thus brought in more income. The women hosted four evening parties each year, planned luncheons for almost any occasion, and held card party benefits for the dual purpose of fun and charity. The final evening party 1935–1936 featured Ping-Pong, bridge, Monopoly, and dancing.

Educational programs were meant to enrich the women's lives with new knowledge, but their purpose was sometimes viewed as social. Explaining the blurred lines between the two, Katherine Humphrey, President from 1926 to 1928, observed in the *Fortieth Anniversary* booklet that "because we were very modern, we did much of our work in the 'Spirit of Play' and some few found it difficult to realize that while many things were labeled 'play' the real purpose was educational."

The increase in social activities, combined with an increase in government-sponsored welfare organizations, caused some to question the Club's role and purpose. In 1937, President Roosevelt initiated the country's Social Security tax to provide income for senior citizens who had been hurt by the Depression. The Woman's Club, as a nonprofit organization existing mainly for charitable purposes, assumed that it would be exempt from this tax. After lengthy correspondence with the Internal Revenue Service, it was decided that because the Club did not exist exclusively for educational or charitable purposes but also as a social organization, it would not be exempt. The social activities that had become so important for keeping the Club together ended up hurting them financially in this new era. This was but a small obstacle; the Club continued to prosper as the country slowly moved out of the Depression.

1714 Chicago Avenue

In 1937, the Club voted to purchase the property and house to the north of the clubhouse, at 1714 Chicago Avenue. Built in 1854, the house was the residence of Evanston's first permanent settlers, John and Hannah Pearsons, and was the first to be built on the block and one of the oldest houses in the city. However, it took the Club three attempts to pass a motion to purchase the property. In the first attempt, less than half the women showed or submitted a proxy, rendering the results inadmissible, and the second attempt was ruled by lawyers to have been an "improper form." Finally, on March 23, 1937, exactly forty-eight years to the day after the first official meeting of the Woman's Club, 756 members voted for purchasing the property, with only 43 voting against it. The Club used its sinking fund to buy the lot, which measured 66 by 210 feet, and its structure for $11,000. As President Isabelle Fowler said, "We now own, clear of debt, 210 by 198 feet on this corner with three buildings. We believe we have acted with wisdom in this matter." The Club used it as a rooming house until it was razed in 1972 and the property leased to the city for a parking lot.

Clubhouse with the house at 1714 Chicago Avenue next door, 1947
CREDIT: EVANSTON PHOTOGRAPHIC STUDIO

Fiftieth Anniversary

*[S]tress must be laid on the notable and significant influence
the Club has had on the members themselves and through
them on their homes. The contact and companionship of the
women, the learning to work together in close harmony, to*

cooperate in all matters for the advancement of humanity, to
put "self" in the background and to gain inspiration from the
rare programs offered during these 50 years, and from the social
intercourse enjoyed at the close of each meeting – all these are
invaluable advantages acquired by its members.

— Harriet Clifton
President, 1911–1913

The women celebrated their fiftieth anniversary at their Annual Luncheon on April 25, 1939. In addition to a pageant titled "The First Fifty Years" featuring the Club's first meeting, the cornerstone, the efforts in the formation of the Auxiliary, Club achievements, and a tribute to their presidents, all active, associate, emeritus, and honorary members were part of the day.

A beautiful commemorative booklet entitled *The Woman's Club of Evanston Fiftieth Anniversary 1939* was printed as a special anniversary issue of the monthly *Bulletin*. This booklet provided a detailed account of the club's history and development for the first fifty years.

Celebrating the 50th Anniversary

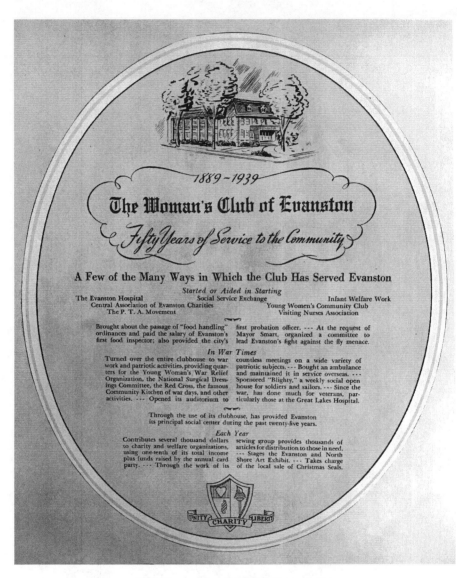

A Few of the Many Ways in Which the Club Has Served Evanston

Started or Aided in Starting

The Evanston Hospital	Social Service Exchange	Infant Welfare Work
Central Association of Evanston Charities		Young Women's Community Club
The P. T. A. Movement		Visiting Nurses Association

Brought about the passage of "food handling" ordinances and paid the salary of Evanston's first food inspector; also provided the city's first probation officer. --- At the request of Mayor Smart, organized a committee to lead Evanston's fight against the fly menace.

In War Times

Turned over the entire clubhouse to war work and patriotic activities, providing quarters for the Young Woman's War Relief Organization, the National Surgical Dressings Committee, the Red Cross, the famous Community Kitchen of war days, and other activities. --- Opened its auditorium to countless meetings on a wide variety of patriotic subjects. --- Bought an ambulance and maintained it in service overseas. --- Sponsored "Blighty," a weekly social open house for soldiers and sailors. --- Since the war, has done much for veterans, particularly those at the Great Lakes Hospital.

Through the use of its clubhouse, has provided Evanston its principal social center during the past twenty-five years.

Each Year

Contributes several thousand dollars to charity and welfare organizations, using one-tenth of its total income plus funds raised by the annual card party. --- Through the work of its sewing group provides thousands of articles for distribution to those in need. --- Stages the Evanston and North Shore Art Exhibit. --- Takes charge of the local sale of Christmas Seals.

Fifty Years of Service to the Community,
1889–1939

The highlight of the booklet was revisiting how the clubhouse itself came to be from initial idea, to raising the money for the building, to the laying of the cornerstone on March 25, 1911, and the opening of the clubhouse on March 11, 1913. According to the booklet, "It is a tribute to the wise financial management in our club to say that the last dollar of indebtedness was paid in 1925," so the clubhouse was paid off and owned free and clear.

Growth during Peacetime

As the women celebrated their fiftieth anniversary, the Club was abuzz with activity. The scrapbooks from 1939 to 1941 are filled with articles and ephemera describing garden tours, teas, luncheons, and bridge parties. The Club held classes on Fridays in subjects such as French and public speaking and showed films on flowers and gardens. The women heard numerous presentations on world affairs, hobbies, ballet, opera, health issues, immigration, travel, table settings, and fine arts. They also kept up to date on the war in Europe which was unfolding on a global scale. Keeping the Club together during the Great Depression proved especially crucial, as the nation was about to enter the Second World War and the women would once again be called upon to serve. The Club accomplished many improvements during the peaceful years including refurbishing the clubhouse in 1940 and revising and rewriting the bylaws in 1941.

The Club invited many women artists and writers to speak. In 1940, Helen Adele Lerch Miller, a well-known sculptor and former associate of the late Lorado Taft, gave a lecture and illustration of her work, and the Club mounted exhibits by painters Pauline Palmer and Helen H. Lawrence. Both the Dramatics Study Group and Club Chorus presented programs, and the Drama Club held joint meetings with the University Guild. Programs presented by members not only showcased their talents but also saved the Club money on entertainment. The Garden Institute was reduced to a one-day event with speakers in the morning and afternoon and judging of floral arrangements during lunch. Summer parties on four Tuesdays drew crowds of up to seven hundred people. The

Evanston Daily News-Index painted a picture of the 1940 Charity Bridge event:

> Up the staircase, past a mammoth white vase of rose
> chrysanthemums on the staircase console, the guests went
> to the bridge tables in the auditorium and lounge. Others
> congregated in the lecture room for the book talk by Mrs.
> Edward L. [May Carney] Middleton. They all had been
> served individual pumpkin pies with whipped cream
> and coffee from tables decorated in huge, shaggy white
> chrysanthemums.

The Club revamped its bylaws in 1939–1940 to put them in a more logical sequence, renovated the clubhouse ventilating system, and bought an electric refrigerator and a fireproof safe in which to store the Club archives. A storage space was renovated in 1939 to provide an on-site office for the president at a cost of $350.

The Club first considered razing the building at 1714 Chicago and either selling or leasing the land to the city for a parking lot in 1940. The need for parking in Evanston's business area had become increasingly critical, and the city had been continually asking the Club for the land. The members, when it was put to a vote, refused, maintaining that it would not be financially beneficial and would lower the clubhouse's property value.

World War II: Leading on the Home Front

As I relinquish the responsibility for the administration of the
affairs of the Club, I bespeak your kind help for the one who
will carry forward the torch of progress. Receive her and her
co-workers with kindness, watch them with patience, and coop-
erate with them with all the goodness in your heart as they as-
sume the leadership of this Club at a critical and difficult hour
in the history of the world.

—Blanche Stevenson Wells
President, 1939–1941

Even before the United States fully entered World War II after the bombing of Pearl Harbor in December 1941, the Club did its part to help those overseas affected by the horrors of war. In addition to keeping informed about events in Europe, the women became very active in Red Cross sewing work. The *Evanston Daily News-Index* from June 2, 1940, reported:

> Memories, two decades old, stirred and translated into
> action by the news flashes of frightful human suffering in
> Europe, have created new interests for the Summer. . . .
> The needs of the American Red Cross, as reported by the
> Evanston chapter, will be weighted by the members of the
> Woman's Club who have had years of training in sewing
> for the unfortunates or underprivileged of peacetime.

Increasing US involvement in the war spurred wartime activities in the Club. In 1940–1941, members devoted Mondays and Thursdays to making surgical dressings for the defense program through the Club's Military Defense Dressing Unit. Hundreds of women were involved, which no doubt provided them a time to come together to discuss their hopes and fears.

Buying and selling war bonds and stamps became a top priority. In May 1942, ten Evanston women joined forces with representatives from other sections of the Chicago metropolitan area to launch a campaign of the USO Women's Division devoted to selling stamps and bonds. Blanche Stevenson Wells (Club President, 1939–1941) served as chair of this group for the entire metropolitan area. Selling these bonds and stamps were integrated into Club activities.

In 1942, Evanston restaurateur Vera McGowan gave a talk on wartime cooking and food shortages in the auditorium. While her presentation was free of charge to the community, she required each attendee to purchase defense stamps that were placed on sale at the door, raising $750. The Club cooperated with the women's division of the War Savings Staff of Evanston by placing booths to sell war bonds and war stamps at businesses all over Evanston, and in March 1943 these booths raised $15,000 in a one-week period. Club members themselves, with private funds, bought $25,000 in bonds and $800 in stamps from one of the Club's booth in the five-month period between December 1942 and April 1943. Club funds were used to buy an additional $14,000 in bonds from 1941–1943. On June 13, 1944, the Minuteman flag was raised in front of the clubhouse, an honor given to clubs and businesses in which more than 90 percent of its members purchased war stamps and bonds.

Beyond sewing garments and selling bonds, the newly formed USO Committee sponsored numerous parties for reserve men and returning soldiers and their spouses at the clubhouse and even turned the first floor west lecture room into a lounge for servicemen who were taking classes on the Northwestern campus. Under the leadership of Ruth Croxton and Corrine Smothers, the Club sponsored a USO Girls' Service Group, made up of women students at Northwestern, to attend parties and be dance partners and hostesses for servicemen along the North Shore. During 1943–1944, this group consisted of four hundred girls, twenty-five chaperones, a registrar, and a transportation chair. The girls attended parties once a month at Fort Sheridan and the Highland Park USO and three times a week at the YMCA. Starting in 1942, buffet suppers were served on the second Sunday of each month for servicemen at the Highland Park USO, which quickly expanded to the Salvation Army USO Center in neighboring Highwood. This successful program continued, with husbands of Club members taking part in serving the food, until gas rationing curtailed the activity.

As the number of returning servicemen increased, the Club sent more flowers, fruits, and other gifts to local hospitals and social service organizations. In cooperation with the Garden Club of Evanston and the Garden Club of the Junior League of Evanston, the Club sent books and flowers to the hospitals at Fort Sheridan and the Naval Training Station in 1941 and the Glenview Naval Air Station and the Great Lakes Naval Station in 1942. In 1942, the Club provided books for the men at the Naval Radio School at Northwestern University and sent cookies, fruit, and candy to cadets. That year, five thousand stockings were filled with gifts for soldiers and WACs as part of the Bundles for America program, and the Club handed out 352 gifts to servicemen and women at a Christmas party held at the service lounge in the Northwestern University Station.

In 1942, the Club's Blood Donor Committee led a registration drive to bring a mobile blood bank to Evanston, which took over the first floor of the clubhouse from August 9 to 13, 1943. Lectures and teas halted so that equipment from the Red Cross could be moved in. Responding to a call for plasma by the Illinois Federation of Women's Clubs, the Club held another drive in 1944. As the Federation's president stated, "the women of Illinois, whose sons might owe their lives to the blood plasma . . . would not want to shirk their personal duty." Further temporary alterations to the clubhouse during World War II included converting the studio room in the basement to an emergency shelter and storing blackout shades, blankets, canned milk, coffee, and tea. The Club donated money to the ambulance fund of the Illinois Federation of Women's Clubs and gave $95 to the Red Cross to prepare kit bags for men going overseas. Educational presentations covered first aid, home hygiene, nursing, nutrition, economics, curtailing expenses, buying bonds, food rationing, and how to grow a victory garden.

As they did during World War I, the women used their positions as wives and mothers to help the families of servicemen. Beginning in 1942–1943, the Club invited wives of military officers to attend regular Tuesday programs and participate in activities for war service such as knitting, making knapsacks, and preparing surgical dressings every Friday afternoon at 2 p.m. The Young Women's Auxiliary opened its activities to younger wives of servicemen who were temporarily stationed in Evanston. This program became so popular that the Club sponsored the Association of Army and Navy Wives and Mothers in January 1943. The association included spouses of those in service regardless of rank; it served as a clearinghouse for information and advice on handling the situations of war, provided programs and entertainment, and acted as a support group.

The Club also established childcare centers in Evanston for women working for the war effort. Helen E. Peterson, chair of the Social Service Department, led a survey in 1943 to assess the community's childcare needs to determine if the number of mothers in need of such service was high enough to warrant federal support. A woman was eligible to register if she had young children and was employed in defense, was taking over the position of a man in the armed services, or if her husband had entered military service. One-third of the children came from families where the father was serving in the armed forces, and the rest had mothers engaged in war-related work. These centers continued beyond the war for families in dire financial circumstances.

While the war raged on, the Club's other activities did not stop. In November 1944, the Club put on a fashion show that included a preview of clothing for postwar plane travel. The Club also held war-themed programs on the first Tuesday of every month during 1943–1944 and organized a victory garden display and exhibit of canned goods in 1942. In 1944, the president of the Club implemented a new project called Adult Education and World Affairs, which she viewed as necessary for well-informed citizenship. Northwestern University professors made presentations on Tuesday mornings on topics that included peace, race relations, Evanston housing conditions and welfare organizations, the spoken word, and household arts.

Service activities outside of the war effort also kept the women busy. They continued selling Christmas seals, collecting change with milk bottles, and cooperating with the Chicago Plant, Flower, and Fruit Guild. In the summer of 1942, the Club helped to send 17,000 bouquets to downtown settlement homes and hospitals. During 1942–1943, the women began holding an annual party for individuals with disabilities, complete with piano music, a dramatic reading, and a comedy skit. The women also sponsored an annual benefit party that helped organizations for people with disabilities, provided memberships to the Emerson Street YMCA, and sponsored new childcare centers.

Building Morale through the Arts

There is too much superficial discussion of vast world problems, and not enough attention paid to the matter of making everyday life more attractive. . . . The Fine Arts Department has tried to keep alive for you some of the beauty of this old world that seems to have few sane moments these days.

—Helen A. Hamilton
Chair, Fine Arts Department, 1940–1941

In addition to the war efforts, the "morale-building relief found in the arts at a time of stress" truly kept the Club together. The women heard talks on the decorative arts, hobbies, beauty, Flemish art, Russian gardens, the philosophy of living, and the use of color in motion pictures. Friday classes remained reserved for courses in the dramatic arts, creative writing, fine arts, and languages. While summer parties were reduced in number from four to three, they were still well attended, and entertainment was provided at meetings and gatherings, including music from the Girls' Choir of Evanston High School.

The Club introduced the Writer's Holiday, a daylong event at which women presented their works from the past year. In 1942, members won five prizes in the annual Tenth District creative writing contest held by the Illinois Federation of Women's Clubs. *Troubadora*, the Club's poetry magazine, first appeared during 1944–1945. Classes and groups existed for nearly every creative activity; the Dramatics Study Group, for example, took an active role in providing entertainment for Club gatherings. Gardening was considered a creative activity, and the members grew victory gardens for the war effort, with joint meetings held between several gardening groups around the North Shore. The Club postponed the 1942–1943 annual art exhibit, but the 1944 exhibit included a War Veterans' Exhibit of watercolors, pastels, and ceramics contributed by veterans who received a monetary award for participation. A student exhibit was held in 1940, featuring works from Evanston Public Schools, the Evanston Academy of Fine Arts, and local studios.

Adjusting to the Changing Needs

Our part as Club women is to be well informed, bring pressure of numbers in support of movements of legislation when we are sure of our position and that our expression of approval or protest will be effective. Another way in which we can all serve effectively as Club women and as citizens is to do all we can in our own homes, our schools, our block, our city, to promote worthy organizations and movements, keep our families well-adjusted and happy, cooperate with our neighbors for the good of the community because, I am convinced, it is by beginning at home in our local situations to make conditions favorable for the best kind of living that we can eventually hope for world order and peace. Being of value to our own community does not preclude giving aid to any group or nation that is in need.

—Marie Vick Swanson
President, 1945–1947

In the war's most critical year of 1944–1945, the Club led a drive to collect clothing for war refugees around the world. Marie Roberts and Doris Hargis collaborated with organizations around Evanston including the Elks' Club, St. Mark's, First Methodist Church, Covenant Methodist Church, and the Russian and British War Relief Clubs to collect enough clothing from Evanston residents to fill two freight cars. In another collaborative effort, Roberts acted as the general chair of Emergency Food Collection in Evanston. Many other women's groups participated, including the South End Woman's Club, Catholic Woman's Club, North End Mothers' Club, and PTA groups, again demonstrating the incredible cooperative spirit of this time. Collection boxes made by the Girl Scouts and College YWCA gathered $2,700 worth of food.

When the war ended in the fall of 1945, the women rejoiced along with the rest of the country, but they also quickly recognized the needs of a postwar society. Under the Club's sponsorship, the Girls Service Organization attended parties for returning servicemen at Fort Sheridan, Great Lakes Naval Academy, the YMCA, and the Highland Park USO. Club members gave parties in private homes for veterans suffering from psychoneurosis or fatigue. Red Cross sewing and preparing surgical dressings continued on Mondays and Thursdays, with an average of twenty-five women per meeting, and the women continued giving gifts to hospital patients. The War Bond and Stamp Committee finally closed its last booth in December 1945, with total proceeds amounting to almost $100,000.

Recognizing the changing needs of its members, the Club endeavored to match Club activities to the members' diversifying interests. It also moved to strengthen internal leadership, holding women accountable for their positions. The Club had reduced its departments to two in the early years of the war (combining Home and Education and Social Services), but increased the number to three after the war's end. Revisions to the by-laws in 1947 required the chair of each department to be nominated by the Nominating Committee and then elected by the Club to the board. The department chairs were further given the power to appoint officers and committee chairs. Membership in individual departments was eliminated, making all the women eligible for any type of activity or service; the stricter rules on leadership ensured that this work continued.

The war had sparked interest in international affairs, as did the formation of the United Nations in October 1945. The women held "armchair tours" of the Philippines, China, Australia, Norway, and India; heard lectures on Iceland, South Africa, and Berlin; and saw films on France and Mexico. They learned about America's place in the changing global landscape from radio commentators, news analysts, and magazine reporters. In 1946, the Club established connections with international students at Northwestern University and invited the students and their spouses, along with Club members' children and husbands, to a party to promote greater understanding.

As intercontinental travel became easier and more convenient, the Club staged fashion shows featuring travel apparel from Marshall Field's and presented films and lectures on bike tours and cruises. The *Fiftieth Anniversary* booklet, published in 1949, indicates that while these events were always met with mixed reviews, they drew a large audience:

> They said it was too frivolous a program, beneath the dignity of "our Woman's Club," to spend a whole afternoon looking at a fashion parade. . . . We needed relaxation, something to laugh about. Besides, the Style Show cost nothing, thus saving funds for something unusually uplifting. It gave us the chance to see fashionable apparel worn by women of the same appearance and taste as ourselves. Others said nothing, but came. The audience was so big that Miss Knaggs had to send for the firemen. They also were entertained and told their wives about it.

Fashion shows only increased in popularity in the decades following World War II and were an early feature of the Auxiliary's popular Benefit Show, which started in 1951.

During this time, the women became more involved with the Girl Scouts. The Club held a demonstration of crafts and other programs for the Scouts. In 1948, the Club donated $350 to the Evanston Girl Scout Summer Camp Fund to install a fireplace in their main lodge in Hills Lake, Wisconsin. The next year, the Club gave $1,000 toward a new Girl Scout Camp at Lake Windego in Wild Rose, Wisconsin.

An annual party for disabled individuals became another regular activity. In 1949, the Club created the Sunshine Club with other Evanston organizations to ensure these parties were of the highest caliber. The women also continued to sell Christmas seals, with 95 percent of the proceeds going to the Evanston Chest Clinic for X-ray screening. The Club raised a record $19,500 for this cause in 1948. The milk bottle collection and money for those in need during the Christmas season were ongoing projects.

All of these activities necessitated some major renovations to the clubhouse. In 1947–1948, two oil burners were replaced, a grand piano was rebuilt, the powder room on the first floor was renovated, and the entire clubhouse interior was cleaned and painted. As a result, the amount from dues that went to maintenance rose from 23 to 25 percent.

Hobby shows, demonstrations, and classes became increasingly popular as women looked for new ways to spend their time after the war ended and they returned to family life. The members also kept informed on legislative issues. On October 19, 1949, the Club and the League of Women Voters invited candidates for the office of the governor, US senator, and representatives for Congress from the Thirteenth District to speak at the clubhouse. A letter from President Corrine Smothers read, "since 51 percent of the voters in the United States are women, it becomes of utmost importance that women use their vote intelligently." Art and social times reigned during the period, but the Club never lost sight of its civic and legal responsibilities.

Family, Home, Peace, and Security

Through our Club, our lives have been enriched by the widening of our horizons, fine comradeship has been enjoyed, a warm spirit of cooperation has been fostered, and communities both at home and abroad have been served in various capacities through our efforts and our philanthropies. The hope is that this all adds up to the furthering of a better understanding of human relations, which is the foundation of World Peace.

—Bertha Kirkpatrick
President, 1949–1951

This postwar American landscape brought a new focus on the family and home. Fear of political uprisings and attacks on American soil caused individuals and groups alike to emphasize security in the nation and in the home. Club activities slowed during these years as women refocused their efforts on their own homes and children. Other organizations gained a stronger foothold in the community, and some women turned their efforts away from the Club to other avenues that would better meet their changing interests. Although it may be true that some members left the Club, according to the *Seventy-Fifth Anniversary* booklet, the Club hummed with activity during 1947–1948. In the following two years, the Club, in cooperation with the Council of Social Agencies and the Health Department of Evanston, paid one-third of the cost of a tuberculosis study in Evanston, distributed milk bottles for collection of cash, furnished a room at the Community Hospital, and started several new projects. The clubhouse was updated with new furnishings, paint, and decoration. The bylaws were revised in 1949–1950, and programs were offered almost every Tuesday as well as bringing in nationally known speakers like Alistair Cooke, Emily Kimbrough, and Richard Armour.

Club members who remained involved became increasingly interested in international cultures and events, especially with the implementation of "armchair globe trotter" tours in 1953 under President Frances Dawson. Journalists, newscasters, and philosophers gave talks on world affairs and foreign policy, covering a wide range of countries that included Egypt, Switzerland, Italy, England, Canada, and more. Parties had international themes as well—for example, Caribbean Cruise Night was the theme of the April 1952 dinner dance. Despite the ongoing Cold War with the Soviet Union, the Club sponsored Art Behind the Iron Curtain in 1951. The Club also sent supplies for Aid for Korea and donated $400 in 1954 to the Korean Orphanage, a project of the Illinois Federation of Women's Clubs. Funds also went to the local Philippine Community Center and the World Council of Churches, and a scholarship fund was set up for international students at the National College of Education.

Protection of the American way of life took center stage during the Cold War era. Talks on finances were incredibly popular during this time, providing the members with information about how to save and invest, thus protecting their money and future. The first of these talks focused on insurance and annuities, and the second on investments.

In this patriotic postwar culture, the Club organized presentations on the protection of citizenship and American culture and contributed $800 to the restoration of Independence Hall, symbolic of the country's need to reaffirm its identity. This amount of money, in addition to an essay contest they held for schoolchildren on "What America Means to Me," earned the Club the State Citizenship Award. Highlighting the decade's focus on the family, the Club introduced programs for husbands. Harriett West, a delegate to the community's civil defense activities (much like home-land security), reminded members that "preparedness is the watchword of Freedom."

Taking Care of the House

Between the 1920s and 1950s, the percent of income from dues allocated to maintenance fluctuated between 20 and 35 percent. Each year, the clubhouse needed more and more repairs and improvements to the roof, chimney, paint, landscaping, decor, drains, and more. In 1954, rental fees (for wedding receptions, dances, benefit parties, and organizational meet-ings) were increased by 10 percent to keep up with all of these costs. The clubhouse continued to hold the members together with a shared sense of identity, and also held the Club together by providing much-needed income.

Membership changed as well: the Junior Committee was created in 1954 for women ages thirty-two to thirty-five to bridge the age gap between the Auxiliary and the Woman's Club. This committee helped the younger women adjust to the larger club and stimulated more of them to enter full active membership.

Volunteering and Fundraising

With the Cold War's focus on family togetherness and homeland protec-tion, and with social service organizations becoming increasingly inde-pendent, women felt they had to justify time spent outside of the home. The Club began tallying volunteer hours and strengthened its ties with established community organizations by appointing members to act as delegates to nearly every social service organization in the community. These delegates reported back to the Club on the organizations' needs for volunteers or funding. In 1959, however, the Club voted to withdraw from membership in the General Federation of Women's Clubs. The Execu-tive Committee minutes for December 8, 1958, indicate that there were concerns regarding the unequal burden of dues to the General Federation falling on the larger women's clubs. Other women's clubs apparently agreed, and it's possible that this was partly behind the vote to withdraw.

When contributing money, the women intended to preserve the dignity of their beneficiaries. For example, the milk bottle campaign, which initially took place in November and December and raised $200–400 each year, was continued through January to provide gifts for the following year—an action that prevented the Holiday Bureau from "having to rely on gifts which, however well-intended, bear the stigma of charity. With cash in his own hand, the beneficiary of the 'Milk Bottle Campaign' gets an extra gift for Christmas—the preservation of his self-respect."

The Club continued to sell Christmas seals until 1951, with 6 percent of proceeds going to the National Tuberculosis Institute and the rest kept locally for the X-ray unit. After a mail carrier stole some of the funds in 1950—which in that year totaled an impressive $20,896.15—the Club decided to discontinue this fundraising activity.

Immediately after terminating its partnership with the Tuberculosis Institute, the Club began sponsoring Evanston's first Mothers March on Polio as part of the March of Dimes campaign. The Woman's Club and Young Woman's Auxiliary cosponsored the march with the cooperation of other Evanston organizations, adding Evanston to the list of more than five hundred communities using this fundraising method. On January 29, 1952, from 7 to 8 p.m., police sirens kicked off the march. Citizens who wanted to contribute money kept their porch light on or tied a handkerchief to their doorknob so that the marching women would stop. To alert residents in advance, advertisements were played before films at the theater and on the radio. "On the coldest and most forbidding night of this year several hundred Evanston Clubwomen spent the hours from early dinner to about midnight going from door to door collecting contributions. . . . The Woman's Club was successful beyond expectations." The Club raised $10,000 in advance donations and another $10,000 during the march. Additional donations brought the total to $23,750 for the first year. According to a 1952 newspaper clipping pasted in the Auxiliary's scrapbook, this first march was notable "because of the determination and enthusiasm of these women, who refused to permit below-zero weather or other obstacles to stand in their way. The community is indebted to them both for bringing the polio fund up to approximately what it should be and for setting an example of effective civic effort." The Club raised $28,401 in 1953 and $23,000 in 1954, a year that also drew nearly 1,700 volunteers. The 1954 campaign raised a total of $35,000—$9,000 more than any other Chicago suburb. That year, Evanston became a test area, where booths were set up at seven businesses around the community to collect advance donations. With a part of the money raised, Ada Deletzke (President, 1961–1963) and Frances Dawson (President, 1953–1955) gave $10,000 to the American Academy of Pediatrics to further the academy's work in pediatric education. After the women raised $20,500 in 1955, less than the previous year and far below their goal, the Club discontinued its affiliation with the march because the money raised fell far short of their goal.

Work with the March of Dimes helped the Club to achieve full nonprofit status (501c3). Rulings in both 1942 and 1943 had deemed that the Club was arranged for primarily social purposes (despite their war efforts), so it had to pay taxes on dues and initiation fees. In 1953, the Club asked the United States Treasury Department to reconsider its decision, citing the Club's leadership role in the Mothers March on Polio campaign in Evanston. A letter dated May 26, 1953, from Norman Sugarman, assistant commissioner of the US Treasury Department, stated that the Club's social activities are "not a material part of its predominate activities or purposes, but are subordinate and merely incidental to its civic, educational and philanthropic activities and purposes." The Club successfully lobbied to have its taxes refunded for the previous four years (per the statute of limitations) and received $16,343 (including interest, some $4,256 went toward legal fees). Following very specific guidelines regarding money received and money spent, the Club remains a nonprofit organization.

After discontinuing its work with the March of Dimes, the Club focused its efforts on raising money for the United Fund, which included a number of different organizations and thus reflected the increasing diversity and interests of the Club members. The Evanston United Fund was created as a result of pressure from large donors who were unhappy that the Community Chest—which received 70 percent of its funding from 7 percent of the local population—was failing to reach its fundraising goal each year. The growth and reputation of the United Fund began to attract large donors, including the Woman's Club. Some members expressed concern that the United Fund was too impersonal, but the ability to raise more funds trumped these fears.

The Club continued its annual benefit party, raising thousands of dollars each year for a variety of charities, and took on new partnerships as the need arose. But even into this new decade, the list of organizations that received contributions reveals long-term partnerships.

In addition to raising money, the women contributed thousands of volunteer hours to the community. In 1950, the Club created a tot lot park and playground on their property to the north of the clubhouse. A survey revealed that two hundred children of preschool age resided within a four-block radius of the clubhouse, and the women wanted to give them a safe place to play. The Club continued to give parties for disabled individuals

1944 Benefit Party program

and senior citizens and to host events and furnish rooms at the Hines and Downey Hospitals for veterans. One room at the Hines hospital "serves as a social and recreation room for the ward, [and] has been completely fitted out with davenports and chairs in modern blond wood with plastic upholstery. Galley figured draperies have been hung at windows on three sides of the room, and a number of large stoker stands and floor laps have been installed." The members understood that beautiful, calming spaces could aid greatly in the healing process. In 1959, the Hospital Committee alone completed 991 hours of service, making bandages and puppets for patients and handling administrative tasks.

Welfare Sewing continued as it had since the early days at Stanwood's home in 1897, providing garments to the Visiting Nurse Association, among others. The Club created the Public Health Committee in 1954–1955 to oversee numerous health-related activities, including the March of Dimes, Mothers March, and the X-Ray Mobile Unit. In addition to the March on Polio, the women took charge of mobilizing Evanston clubwomen to spread the word about a mobile blood bank on December 5 and 6, 1951. Marjorie Weaver, Rita Miner, Agnes Asker, and Alice Whitfeld of the Social Service Department contacted forty-six Club presidents and convinced them to help with advertising and staffing the bank. Despite ceasing the sale of Christmas seals, the Club annually staffed a monthlong volunteer-run X-ray Mobile Unit in Evanston throughout the 1950s to screen for tuberculosis. The unit was set up in late August and operated through the month of September. The Club and Auxiliary were also two of twenty-three cooperating organizations to pursue a community tuberculosis survey in 1956.

Staying Strong by Enduring

During this period the Club focused more on placing delegates in the social service organizations that were becoming firmly established, in part to maintain connections within the community. The Woman's Club in many ways linked all of these organizations together by enabling the delegates to exchange ideas and keep up with the activities of other organizations so that duplication of efforts could be avoided. Further, delegates kept Club members informed on the most pressing issues in the community and the world. This strategy also helped to maintain cohesiveness in the Club when the needs of other organizations were pulling members away.

While Tuesdays were Club program days, Fridays featured a program by the Special Interests Committee with an informal hour that followed. Classes were offered in bridge, dressmaking, millinery, writing, Spanish, dance, and such activities as flower arranging, weaving, interior decorating, painting, and ceramics. The Collectors Group began during 1954–1955 to facilitate and support antique collecting. Functioning under the Home and Education Department, this group brought women together to discuss antiques, tour museums, and display the collections in their homes. An annual all-group exhibit was held at the clubhouse each February. The house tours and the annual exhibit were themed, for example, "Lamps through the Ages," "My Favorite Heritage Pieces" (1973), and "Treasures from the Past" (1976).

Around this time, committees began to assume greater importance than departments. Home and Education and Fine Arts broke apart into separate committees. Although the Social Science Department remained very active, the Public Health Committee also attracted much attention. Committees allowed the members to pursue more specific interests in a smaller group setting. Embracing diversity kept the membership strong: the Woman's Club of Evanston at this time was one of only twelve clubs in the state of Illinois with more than five hundred members.

After the prosperity of the Roaring Twenties, the women had been through the Great Depression, a Second World War, and now the Cold War, yet they still held a waiting list for membership of fifty to one hundred women and continued to serve the community in a variety of ways.

CHAPTER FOUR

"Times They Are A'Changing":
1960s through the 1980s

*The strength and accomplishments of our Club are not
only due to each President and the devoted and energetic
service given by the Board members and committees but that
strength also comes from the membership, as a whole, whose
concern and participation have helped us meet the challenge
of changing times. . . . So it is that we who represent the
past, and those who represent the present, look forward with
confidence to the future.*

—Ruth Erickson
President, 1957–1959

The social change and technological advances of the 1960s and '70s
brought new challenges to the Woman's Club of Evanston. Social roles
were shifting, with issues of gender and race constantly up for question
and redefinition. Women working outside of the home became common-
place as the Club entered the 1970s, and the influence of second-wave
feminism developed a wide reach. The civil rights movement and the
United States' participation in the Vietnam War led to a sharp rise in student and community unrest. "Never in the history of this nation have we
faced the tasks that are before us now. . . . We cannot sit back and bemoan
what is happening. We must become better informed, more articulate,
and effective," expressed Elizabeth Mueller (President, 1969–1971) in
the *Bulletin*. As a result, the Club underwent numerous membership and
structural changes in order to meet the changing needs of the Evanston
community and the changing demographics of the Club.

THE WOMAN'S CLUB
OF EVANSTON

75
SPARKLING
YEARS

1889–1964

75th Anniversary Booklet

Addressing a Declining Membership

*When we look ahead to the coming year and beyond it, we
know that we will be faced with new conditions and new
demands. Our adjustment to these changes will determine
our future. Our theme for this year has been a very timely
one— "Today Decides Tomorrow's Destiny." It emphasizes the
importance of every step we take and every decision we make.*

—Marian Waitley
President, 1963–1965

Due to increasing financial difficulties, and obligations to the home and community, membership decreased each year. The Club went from 975 active members in 1961 to 500 by 1975, and by 1996 there were fewer than 300 active members. However, membership in the Young Woman's Auxiliary increased from 188 in 1961 to 223 in 1975.

Members did everything they could to welcome new women—holding twice-yearly new member orientations and setting up a new member/hospitality table at each monthly luncheon. Members were encouraged to wear nametags whenever possible and always introduce themselves to potential and new members. "If we may repeat here what might be called our theme song for these past two years it is this: In order to have friends, one must first be a friend; and make the Woman's Club a place where you speak to someone new each time you are present and remember to greet her when next you meet," said Ada Deletzke, President from 1961 to 1963, in her annual report.

But employment and the demands of home life, the growth of other social service organizations and agencies, an aging membership, and newly gained rights for women made increasing and retaining membership difficult. A 1979 news article placed in the Club's scrapbook emphasized the shift in priorities: "The Club, founded in 1889, clings to its Tuesday daytime meetings, whereas its Auxiliary has chosen a 'mixed bag' of gatherings, morning, noon, and evening, to meet the needs of its younger members who are returning to work or to school. Women's organizations are faced with the continued threat of decreasing membership by rescheduling meetings and beefing up social issues and community service programs." The Club continually reexamined its policies and activities to ensure that its network would be in place for future generations to reap its benefits.

The Young Woman's Auxiliary became extremely active during these decades, and the Club worked to bridge the gap between the two groups. In 1981, the Auxiliary tested a one-year term for its president. This allowed the Club and the Auxiliary to learn more about each other's activities. The one-year term became official in 1983, pushing the members to pursue more goals in shorter time periods and increasing communication among all members. This change also encouraged members whose busy schedules would not allow a two-year commitment to run for this office.

Contributions

1956—total amount $1,837.00

Orchard School for Retarded Children
Community Hospital
Cleft Lip and Palate Institute
North Shore Assn. for Retarded Children
Mary Bartelme Club
Evanston Hospital Out-Patient Clinic

1957—total amount $3,280.00

Community Hospital
Evanston Y.M.C.A.
Chicago Diabetes Assn.
North Shore Assn. for Retarded Children
Evanston Hospital Out-Patient Clinic
Park Ridge School for Girls
Evanston Day Nursery
Levinson Foundation
Brain Research

1958—total amount $2,850.00

Chicago Diabetes Assn.
Evanston Day Nursery
Evanston Hospital Out-Patient Clinic
Community Consolidated Schools
Evanston Y.M.C.A.
Cleft Lip and Palate Institute
Orchard School
Brain Research
Evanston Center For Older People

1959—total amount $2,973.00

Chicago Diabetes Assn.
Cerebral Palsy of Chicago
Visiting Nurses Assn.
J. R. Skiles Revolving Fund
Family Service of Evanston
Community Hospital
Evanston Y.M.C.A.
Evanston Center For Older People
Cancer Research at Evanston Hospital
Levinson Foundation

1960—total amount $2,446.86

Chicago Foundlings Home
Cleft Lip and Palate Institute
Family Service Bureau
Hadley School for the Blind
Institute of Language and Hearing Disorders of N.U.
Mental Health Society of Greater Chicago

St. Leonard's House
West Side Christian Parish Youth Center
Community Hospital
National Foundation
Evanston's Children's Home of Illinois Children's
   Home and Aid Society

1961—total amount $4,000.34

Cleft Lip and Palate Institute of N.U.
Levinson Research Foundation
Evanston Hospital Cancer Research Fund
North Shore Assn. for Retarded Children

1962—total amount $3,130.15

Brain Research Foundation, Inc.
St. Leonard's House
North Shore Assn. for Retarded Children
West Side Christian Parish
Scholarship and Guidance Assn.
Institute for Language Disorders
Child Care Association

1963—total amount $4,260.00

Levinson Foundation
Shore School and Training Center
Cancer Chemotherapy Research

1964—total amount $5,500.00

Ridge Farm
St. Francis Hospital Adult and Child Guidance Center

1965—total amount $6,543.00

Family Counseling Service
St. Francis Hospital Adult and Child Guidance Center

1966—total amount $9,040.00

The Fund for Perceptually Handicapped Children
St. Francis Hospital Adult and Child Guidance Center

1967—total amount $11,080.00

The Lambs, Inc.
Evanston Hospital Evaluation Center For Learning
   Problems

1968—total amount $14,616.18

The Child Care Center of Evanston
The Volunteer Bureau of Evanston

YWA Contributions Recap 1955–1968

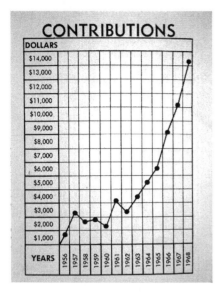

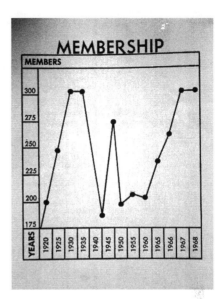

CREDIT: YWA ANNIVERSARY BOOKLET

The Club and Auxiliary had collaborated on major projects in the past, such as the Mother's March on Polio, staffing the tuberculosis mobile X-ray unit, and the Christmas seals drive. Now they expanded their pursuit of joint projects, such as the production of the *Once Upon a Thyme* cookbook in 1982. More than ever, the Club realized that its continued existence depended on reaching out to this next generation of leaders. To facilitate this process, the Club designated its first Auxiliary relations officer in 1982 to attend meetings and events of the Auxiliary, seek out and create collaborative opportunities, and report back to the Club. "The Board of Directors recognized the value of working closely with our Auxiliary members in the sense of partnership," the *Bulletin* stated. "The Club's Auxiliary Relations Committee was expanded to include members from both groups; Auxiliary members were encouraged to actively participate on such committees as Parties and The Collectors; the experimental concept of an Auxiliary Representative to the Club board has evolved into an officer of the Auxiliary serving as liaison in an expanded role and sitting upon the Club board in an official capacity."

To keep the younger members active in the Club, both the Junior Committee and Young Woman's Auxiliary provided babysitting services for daytime events and meetings. The age requirements for the progression from the Auxiliary to the Junior Committee to the Woman's Club underwent revisions. In 1965, the Junior Committee was changed to encompass women ages 32 to 37. In 1970, it expanded the range to include women up to age 40, while the Young Woman's Auxiliary range was set at age 32 and younger. Women were eligible to leave the Junior Committee and become full members of the Woman's Club once they reached membership age. In 1978, the Junior Committee was eliminated. As a result of this change, any woman who had been an Auxiliary member for seven years or more was now eligible to join the Woman's Club rather than waiting until she was 40. In 1987, to accommodate an aging membership and solidify friendships and bonds between the women, the Club raised the Auxiliary's age limit to 41. When the Auxiliary was dissolved in 1999, its age limit had reached 45.

By 1993, over half of the members held part-time or full-time jobs, and among the members there were 251 children. The Auxiliary further accommodated this increasing number of working members by alternating meetings between daytime and evening hours and, in 1986, changed the annual luncheon to an annual dinner. The September 1975 Auxiliary newsletter announced, "Attention all night owls and working girls . . . Have we got a YEAR planned for YOU!!! (in the EVENING)!" Meetings, parties, volunteer projects, and Benefit Show rehearsals were moved to the evening, a benefit not only to women in the workforce but also to stay-at-home mothers. The Auxiliary newsletters from this period provide a sense of the delicate work-family-life balance that many of these women were determined to achieve and the importance that children and family played in members' lives. Programs and presentations about how best to raise children had appeared frequently on the Club calendar for nearly its entire existence, and these topics remained popular. For example, in January 1985, the Auxiliary learned how to "modify undesirable behavior by positive reinforcement techniques." The numerous birth announcements, anywhere from two to ten, published in each monthly newsletter reinforced the importance of family. This section of the Auxiliary newsletter also offered news about members' new jobs, moves across town or across the country, vacations, and more, and all new Auxiliary members were featured with a brief biography.

Despite these efforts, membership in the Auxiliary, and by consequence the Club, continued to diminish during the 1970s. The Club's membership continued to age, while the Auxiliary's ability and enthusiasm for community service held steady, so the women sought ways to maintain the membership levels of the Auxiliary and bring graduating Auxiliary members into the Club. In the 1970s, the Auxiliary initiated an inactive member status for women who needed time off to juggle the demands of work and family life, which kept membership numbers steady. In 1987, the Auxiliary created a sustaining level of membership for women who could not commit to full participation but still wished to be affiliated, bringing much-needed income to the Club. In 1986, the Auxiliary created the Woman's Club relations officer to further ease the transition from Auxiliary to Club life and to encourage member retention.

As it had for decades, the Club continued to provide a variety of membership levels, including associate (residing within a 25-mile radius), nonresident (residing outside of a 25-mile radius), inactive members, emeritus members, and honorary members, in addition to the active members. By 1980, the Club had set up a prorated fee schedule so that women could join at any time of the year without penalty. By the late 1980s, the membership limit was set at 800 active members. As revealed through letters found in the archives, not all members agreed with the demographics or dues, some finding the dues too steep and the membership boundaries closed to individuals of different backgrounds. "I believe it is time for the Evanston Women's Club to establish open membership," one letter read. "Evanston's sisterhood, including religious and ethnic minorities, are also Evanston women. In fact, I believe that Evanston as a cosmopolitan community has many women who could add immensely to the strength and variety of our Club." A 1989 *Chicago Tribune* article about the Club noted: "To survive, clubs must attract young women, especially members of minority groups." In keeping with the Club's original intent to draw on different perspectives and knowledge systems to achieve what is best for the community, the Club worked to ensure that its membership reflected Evanston's diversity.

Adapting by Creating New Traditions

Despite the fact that property taxes and insurance costs doubled in 1979, the members' financial skills kept the budget balanced. The Club also saved money by changing traditions and altering services where it could. When the mold of the president's pin was lost and deemed prohibitively expensive to replace, the Club started a new tradition of obtaining past presidents' pins for the new presidents to wear, thus creating a link with the Club's past. The monthly *Bulletin* became a bimonthly newsletter in 1984, saving the Club almost $2,000 that year. Also in 1984, the Club changed the beginning of its fiscal year from May 1 to June 1. Some members expressed concern that many women perceived the Club year as falling between October and April, which put the Antiques Show, held in May, at a disadvantage. Changing the fiscal year put more focus on the event, allowed more time for processing late payments and invoices, and sped up the Club's annual audit.

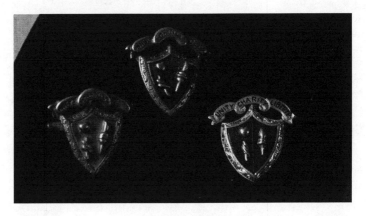

President's pins

The Changing Social Landscape

We have shown the activities of the Woman's Club illustrated perhaps as in balance on a scale—a balance between programs and services, all of which fall in the field of hospitality and friendship and joy in association in which areas we have made great effort to help each of you enjoy your Club membership.

—Ada Deletzke
President, 1961–1963

The Club continued its educational and creative programs, choosing a different theme each year. A few examples include *The Bridge of Under-standing*, which was the theme in 1960–1961, *It Is When You Give of Yourself That You Truly Give* in 1977–1978, *Values Are Nurtured by Responsibility* in 1982–1983, and *Participation Is Essential for Progress* in 1985–1986. Program topics covering travel, home décor, gardening, music, and holidays were presented along with more serious topics such as world affairs and national defense, which reflected the social unrest at home and abroad. In 1963, the delegate to the School of World Affairs, an organization that the Club had helped start in the 1920s, reported a rapid decline in SWA membership, which she speculated was due in part to the increasing use of radio and television to gather news. The Special Inter-ests Committee and their Friday classes were as popular as ever, providing lessons in oil painting, yoga, ballroom dancing, needlepoint, and creating miniature rooms. Dramatic productions staged both by Club members and by outside groups, musical performances, and book reviews remained popular features, and a joint meeting with the University Guild continued to be planned annually.

The Annual Art Exhibit also remained on the calendar in these decades, drawing work from numerous local artists. The 1974 exhibit attracted twelve thousand attendees and nearly two hundred entrants "despite a blizzard and gas shortage," as was noted in the *Bulletin*. The exhibit, which the press referred to in the 1980s as the Club's "gift to the community," continued to display more than two hundred works of art and draw a thousand guests per show. In 1987, it was moved to the fall to relieve pressure on volunteers and on the clubhouse, which had an over-crowded spring schedule.

Social functions became even more important as the Club sought to increase membership. Monthly luncheons, benefit luncheons, and lun-cheons to honor individual members were held, an example being the cel-ebration of the one-hundredth birthday of Mrs. Edith Fowler, President of the Club from 1935 to 1937. In January 1976, the Club began having mini luncheons, which became a weekly occurrence in the 1980s. These are described in the archives as working lunches, where the committees met to discuss their work and listen to educational programs, but they also provided a time when working women were able to get together. The Club held bridge gatherings on the first Friday of each month, along with morning coffee hours and dessert parties throughout the year to acquaint new members with the Club. A glance at the calendar for 1973 shows the Club was holding brunches, coffee hours in the summer, and teas throughout the year and after events. The traditional annual luncheon at the end of the Club year gave members an opportunity to celebrate the Club's accomplishments. Dances were held twice a year, once at Christmas and once in the spring. The President's Reception marked the opening of the new Club year every other October to introduce the new Club president to members and community leaders. The Young Woman's Auxiliary held its own benefit dinner and dance parties—called Benefit Backers—from 1973 to 1990 in order to raise funds for the Benefit Show. In 1982, a silent auction was added to the event to boost proceeds. In the early 1990s, the members transformed this event into a dinner dance to raise money for a single charity recipient. All of these activities, including the well-attended guest night, continued throughout the 1980s. Records show that in 1985, more than five thousand individuals attended these luncheons, parties, and programs.

President's Reception receiving line, 1966
CREDIT: EVANSTON PHOTOGRAPHIC STUDIOS

Due to financial constraints, the women were not always able to meet their own standards of décor at these gatherings. Evidence of the ongoing effort behind the scenes of these events can be found, for example, in the Floral Committee report in 1965 that noted: "Our budget for the year was only $200, making it impossible to buy sufficient materials for any unusual arrangements . . . it has been suggested that the number of tea tables be reduced from three to two and that a permanent arrangement or decorative object be obtained for the foyer to eliminate this responsibility each week." The year 1975 saw only one dance, at Christmastime, the Snow Ball. In 1976, the Club president asked, "What woman's club could operate without flowers?" All Club events required much attention to detail and advance planning. The chairs of the committees had to come up with creative ways (e.g., reducing the number of tables or permanent flower displays) to offset the financial constraints.

As the Club decreased in size, programs were consolidated under an overarching Programs Committee that worked in consultation with the departments to plan the year's schedule. The program chair of this committee functioned as the contractual agent for all of the Club's programming, working with outside vendors and handling fees for paid speakers. The Public Health and Welfare Committee took over community service, and the Contributions Committee handled fundraising and charitable distributions. The Club became more streamlined and businesslike in the 1970s and '80s as it changed to meet the needs of their members and the community.

Community Service Remains a Stalwart

The Woman's Club of Evanston has been an important force in Evanston affairs for eighty-one years. It has seen epochal periods of change in the community environment in which it exists and to which it contributes. Its challenge in the decade ahead is to move forward and to expand its concept of community service to be in tune with this rapidly changing times without sacrificing the values that have been built in its distinguished history.

—Mrs. Marion Peirce
President, 1969–1971

The Club continued to volunteer and raise funds for charitable and welfare organizations. The Public Health Committee became the Public
Health and Welfare Committee in 1960 and assumed control of nearly
all Club volunteer projects, while the Social Services Department took
charge of programming and the annual benefit party. The women concentrated their efforts in a few particular areas, increasing collaboration
among members to carry out larger projects.

As they had for decades and through multiple wars, the women served
the needs of veterans by arranging entertainment programs and contributing gifts to Downey Veteran Administration Hospital. They also contributed thousands of volunteer hours each year at Evanston Hospital,
servicing the book cart, working in the coffee shop, delivering flowers,
and managing the family lounge.

Members continued their long-standing tradition of sewing up to four
hundred garments each year for the Visiting Nurse Association, eventually concentrating on making layettes (outfits) for infants. Other organizations that benefited from their sewing included Evanston School
Children's Welfare, Evanston Hospital, and the Indian Mission. During
1973–1974, the Club set up sewing machines in the West Room on the
second Thursday of each month for members to work together creating
garments in a collaborative and supportive setting. The Philanthropy
Committee of the Young Woman's Auxiliary created a collaborative quilt
in 1982 to auction off at the 1983 benefit, and as Donna Brown (Auxiliary President, 1990–1991) recalled, "you can understand how those of
us who constructed pieces and then sat at the quilt stretcher at a shop
in Wilmette could spend a whole morning hand stitching and sharing
stories there never would have been time for at a regular committee
function."

The Club expanded its work with senior citizens during these decades.
In 1962, the tot lot that had served the burgeoning population of children
in the downtown Evanston area in earlier times was turned into a senior
citizen park and garden, and the women sponsored an annual senior citizen volunteer tea that honored some one hundred individuals each year.
The annual Sunshine Party continued, drawing an increasing number of
attendees each year; the records for 1968 indicate there were 212 guests.
In 1972–1973, the women became active participants in the Evanston
Meals at Home program, which delivered meals to those confined by

YWA Collaborative Quilt, 1982

illness or disability, sending volunteers four days a month to help pack
meals at St. Francis Hospital and deliver them around the community.
The Club started Operation Christmas Goodies in 1973–1974, reprising
their efforts in the 1930s to deliver baskets of goods to low-income families at Christmastime. During its first year, the women baked 325 dozen
cookies and packaged them along with fruit and candy canes for delivery
to the Evanston Welfare Department.

The Delegates Committee remained active in the early 1960s, sending members to the Evanston Art Center, Civil Defense, Evanston Center for Senior Activities, Evanston Human Relations Council, Evanston School of World Affairs, Evanston Welfare Council, American Indian Welfare, Junior Achievement, Public Health, Safety Council, School Caucus, School Districts 65 and 202, Social Welfare, the YWCA, Northwestern University, Veterans' Service, and Youth Conservation. However, the number of delegates rapidly decreased until, in 1979, the committee was abolished when the Club determined that its existence was no longer valid. The school caucuses, for example, had disbanded years before, and the groups to which they were delegates could now function on their own. Women still attended meetings of United Community Services and the Evanston Preservation Commission, but they acted in the capacity of representatives rather than as delegates.

In 1977 the clubhouse opened its doors to the Preservation Commission's Historical Field Survey, which gathered data about buildings around town to develop preservation and conservation programs in Evanston. Several women from the Club volunteered to collect information.

In 1983, the women began volunteering at the Terra Museum, which is no longer in existence. And in 1988, twenty-one members joined the docents group of the Evanston History Center Flea Market.

During these decades, the members streamlined their volunteer activities, allowing the Club to provide better and more focused service to those in need. The aging demographics of the Club made it much more difficult for its members to get out and volunteer as often as they once could. The Auxiliary, on the other hand, increased its community service considerably. According to records in the archives, community service projects proliferated in the 1980s. A wide variety of projects were offered to meet the needs and schedules of Auxiliary members. Informal baking projects held at the clubhouse were very popular. These evenings, known as Bake-A-Nights, provided camaraderie as well as purpose. Food items baked during the evenings were donated to a number of shelters. The Auxiliary cuddled drug-addicted babies at Cook County Hospital, served food at Evanston soup kitchens, escorted senior citizens to the Ice Capades, and staffed the Evanston Art Center Holiday boutique. Delivery of Meals at Home continued on Thursdays of each month. By 1989, each Auxiliary member participated in at least three projects per year.

This diversification and multiplication of volunteer activities reflected the Auxiliary's increasingly diverse membership and interests. By offering different kinds of activities, the Auxiliary could appeal to more women and retain its members. Short-term projects, some taking as little as a few hours over one evening, allowed working women, who were now the majority of the membership, to contribute what they could on their own schedules. The Auxiliary had a community service requirement which ensured that each woman contributed at her fullest potential and that the Auxiliary remained relevant in the community.

Increasing Philanthropic Impact

With the loss of membership and increased cost of living, the Club's income from dues and rentals was falling, reducing the amount the Club could contribute to the community. To address this problem, in 1968, the Club created the Woman's Club of Evanston Charitable Foundation, Inc., a 501(c)(3) organization that encouraged members to donate money directly to the foundation and receive a charitable tax deduction. This measure helped the Club meet its philanthropic goals while still being able to support programming and clubhouse maintenance. All Club members were members of the Charitable Foundation, but no foundation trustee served on the Club's board. Based on the decisions of its Board of Trustees, the Charitable Foundation made donations to community organizations in an amount equal to at least 10 percent of the Woman's Club's income from initiation fees and Club and Auxiliary dues, a long-standing obligation stated in the Club's bylaws. Donors could request that their contribution go to a specific charity (in their name), which facilitated the process of donating money in memoriam or leaving money to the Club in one's estate. The foundation made a memorial contribution to Evanston Hospital for every deceased member of the Club and provided supplies to the Welfare Sewing Committee. The goal of the Charitable Foundation was to establish an endowment fund that would provide enough interest earnings to allow the Club to meet its philanthropic commitments. To kick off the fund, the women replaced the benefit party in 1968 with a stay-at-home party that encouraged members to donate directly to the foundation.

Club events continued to focus on philanthropy, with the women holding successful card party benefits and fashion shows to raise money for charities across Evanston and the Chicago area. To celebrate Evanston's centennial—the town was founded in 1863 and incorporated as a city in 1892—the women organized a benefit called A Century of Fashions in October 1963 to highlight women's clothing styles from the past one hundred years. The benefit raised $2,068 for the Park Ridge School for Girls, North Shore Association for Retarded Children, Evanston Community Hospital, Cove School for Perceptually Handicapped Children, and the Senior Citizens Park.

Smaller fashion shows raised money for clubhouse maintenance. One example was the Fabric Frolic luncheon, which took place several times during the 1970s and featured apparel sewn and modeled by Club members. Another example, from 1963, was a benefit party with the theme Carriages to Capsules, which told the story of the building of the clubhouse fifty years earlier, raising $2,671. The 1974 fall Benefit Show, In Touch with Fashion, featured the latest styles from Bonwit Teller, a luxury department store. The 1979 spring benefit, With the Winds of Fashion, featured fashions from Saks Fifth Avenue. Starting in 1975, the Club had two official annual benefit parties, originally organized by the Social Services Department. The Programs Committee took over in 1978 for a couple of years, and then the Club created a Benefit Committee in 1980. That year's recipient was the Visiting Nurse Association, with the funds used for their Home Care for the Dying program. While benefits in past decades had designated the proceeds to benefit several charities, by the mid-1970s the funds usually went to only one organization. In 1977, for example, the spring benefit party and fashion show raised funds to purchase a $1,595 heart-lung resuscitator for the Evanston First Emergency Ambulance. Once again, in lieu of a benefit party during 1969, the women decided to hold a stay-at-home party and asked directly for donations to the Woman's Charitable Foundation Inc. The members opted for something similar in 1970–71 with an appeal for a share-in for funds rather than holding a benefit. The 1980 fall benefit purchased a kiln for the arts and crafts room at the Illinois Children's Home and Aid Society, a longtime Woman's Club charity recipient.

The Club also pursued other types of fundraising campaigns. In 1961, the Club began to raise money for the public television station WTTW.

That year, twenty-one members manned fundraising tables at eight banks and departments stores for twelve hours, with Evanston Junior High students contributing posters, and collected $647.85. In addition to large welfare and educational organizations, the Club also supported smaller, more personal causes. For example, in 1960, the Club created a music scholarship for a high school student to attend a three-week course in Northwestern University's Summer High School Orchestra and Band program. That year, money also went to the Indian Welfare Center, to a campaign to eliminate obscene literature from news stations, toward promotion of Civil Defense and Safety, to the Park Ridge School for Girls and the YWCA, and to support delegates to school caucuses.

The Auxiliary had sponsored an annual benefit and style show for many years. In 1941, the benefit featured an afternoon of dessert luncheon, bridge, a book review and style show. In 1950, the annual philanthropy party and fashion show raised money for the benefit of twenty-one charities. The Auxiliary, however, celebrated their first rehearsed show in 1951, a benefit titled *Vogue Varieties*, "an around-the-clock style show."

YWA members practicing for the Benefit Show, circa 1950s

This event rapidly developed into something even more ambitious. The following year's show, *Paris Calling*, was a musical and style show "with a French setting to provide the mood, the latest in fall fashions for a luxurious touch, and a homespun talent for the spice." Husbands, who discovered that "there's no rest for the male side of the family when their wives become involved in a charity show," were recruited to participate in their fourth show, The Gilded Stage. Over the following decade, the performance aspect of the Benefit Show overshadowed the fashion show, but fashion shows remained on the Club's calendar in the fall months.

In 1975, the Auxiliary created a Benefit Show program book, also called the ad book, which helped them increase proceeds considerably. The book, which has become a Club tradition, contained photos of members and — more importantly — advertisements from local businesses. The ads also featured messages of congratulations and well wishes from these businesses and drew the attention of both local and national politicians and leaders. In a letter included in the ad book for the 1976 production "Red, White, & Whew," US President Gerald Ford wrote: "I am pleased to learn that this year makes the 25th anniversary of your Auxiliary's musical revue. . . . The undertaking of this worthy endeavor represents the kind of generous spirit which leads to a better world for all mankind. I commend you for your long and dedicated work on behalf of your community's service organizations." The Benefit Show garnered press and publicity unlike any other Club event had had for decades, as evidenced by the hundreds of newspaper articles and photos in the Auxiliary's scrapbooks.

In 1965, the Benefit Show was the Auxiliary's only charitable fundraising event, "having grown from a fashion show to a full-scale musical revue involving a full year's planning," but this changed in the 1970s. The Auxiliary ran a project called Granny's Attic in the late 1960s through the 1970s, reminiscent of the work the Club had done with the Thrift House in the 1920s. Calls for goods (except books, records, shoes, and underwear) went out each summer, and the resulting large-scale garage sale was held in places throughout the community, such as the Sigma Alpha Epsilon's headquarters and the Child Care Center. Proceeds ranged anywhere from $4,000 to $9,000. The endeavor ended in 1980, the year the Auxiliary held the first of its popular house walks, a fundraiser featuring tours of several historic homes in Evanston. The house walks continued into the 1990s.

Merry Merry Market, featuring local artisans and businesses selling their wares for the Christmas season, began in 1987 and raised thousands of dollars in admission fees. In the 1960s, the Auxiliary organized Shop and Share days at local supermarkets, a decades-long practice through which the Woman's Club of Evanston received five percent of a shopper's purchase when they presented a designated slip to the cashier. Top shoppers received prizes such as lunch and free admission to the Merry Merry Market. Overall, as noted in the Young Women's Auxiliary *Seventy-Fifth Anniversary* booklet, the Auxiliary as well as the Club made it a point to provide funding to "many different local agencies, often to those who did not receive support from national organizations like the United Way. The Auxiliary usually stipulated the contributions be earmarked for a particular need rather than for general operation expenses."

Although the Benefit Show proceeds were divided among multiple organizations, they shared some common threads. Many of the organizations were devoted to the care of children, health care (both physical and mental), the arts, and the environment. The charter members' original mission of making the world a more fit place to live and ensuring that all are cared for never wavered. The members adapted to the times and supported organizations that met new needs as they arose. Domestic violence is a case in point; as it became a more acknowledged social issue, the Auxiliary responded by contributing money and volunteer hours to this cause, earning the Life Span Community Award, given to organizations with a "demonstrated commitment to the elimination of domestic violence," in 1988.

The Auxiliary published its first cookbook, *Specialties of the House*, in 1967, with a follow-up in 1972 called *A Matter of Course: Favorite Recipes of the Young Woman's Auxiliary of the Woman's Club of Evanston*. Their most popular cookbook, *Once Upon a Thyme*, was published in 1983. The Auxiliary received seven hundred recipe entries and tested each with the help of a professional dietician and cooking teacher at the YMCA. They also collected oral histories and did some research at the Evanston History Center to intersperse a little history of Evanston amid the recipes. As editor Lynne Hoos explained in a Club scrapbook, they wanted to provide "a souvenir book of historic Evanston coupled with an unusual and appealing recipe collection." To add a more professional tone, the authors of the recipes were not named in the cookbook. The compiling of the book was not without its mishaps. Donna Brown, a guest speaker at the President's Dinner, some years later recalled: "it wasn't until our first printing that we discovered the barbeque sauce called for ¼ cup of Tabasco sauce. . . . Sandy Herman actually made it this way and her husband, Peter, who liked spicy food, reportedly had hiccups on and off for several days. Needless to say, the human eye had missed a few details and a correction sheet was printed."

The cookbook, with an image of the Grosse Point lighthouse on the cover, cost $25,000 to produce and was sold at the clubhouse, Hoos Drugstore, and many other places in Evanston and Chicago for $11.95. The Club and Auxiliary held a brunch on Sunday, March 4, 1984, at the Orrington Hotel, featuring recipes from the cookbook and tours of the newly renovated hotel. It received write-ups in the *Chicago Tribune*, and by January 1985 it had sold out, not to be reprinted until 1989. Profits from the book totaled $14,000, which were used to set up a scholarship for Evanston Township High School students who showed a commitment to community service, to refurbish the clubhouse nursery, and to purchase an ice machine.

YWA Cookbook, 1984

Throughout their history, both the Club and the Auxiliary had been questioned about their true purpose in the community, especially in later decades when so many social service organizations and agencies were funded through government sources and grants. The Woman's Club and Auxiliary not only adapted to these changing conditions but also helped other organizations to adapt as well. Their contributions ensured that the organizations they supported would continue to grow and meet the needs of the changing community.

This Old House

The members worked hard to restructure their finances so that they could maintain their support of community organizations at the level they had in the past; however a number of factors made this difficult. The club-house reached the fifty-year-old mark in 1963 and required additional maintenance not only to meet the needs of the Club but to ensure it was structurally sound and safe for use. The Club undertook two major renovations in the 1960s. The kitchen was moved to the first floor from the basement and enlarged and updated, becoming the first addition to the clubhouse since it was built. A report from the Kitchen Planning Committee noted that the kitchen was originally built for five hundred members, not one thousand, which was currently the limit, and that it saw forty thousand uses per year. Further, complying with the city's fire code would be impossible if the kitchen remained in the basement. Moving it upstairs eliminated the need for the dumbwaiters, which were considered a fire hazard. The committee raised the $15,000 needed by asking members to participate in a subscription donation of $1 per month for fifteen months. The Club took $20,000 from the sinking fund and hired architect Edward M. Tourtelot to complete the job.

In 1965, the president's notebook mentions that "consideration was being given to the improvement of the front entrance of the Club to include a new driveway and almost a completely new entrance." The driveway needed to be widened to accommodate the growing size of automobiles, and the front entrance need to be updated to improve the member and guest experience: "designed in 1912, the steps are too steep and the driveway not adequate for today's longer motor cars." The Club used

Front porch construction, 1960s

$15,000 from the sinking fund and raised an additional $20,000 from members. In 1970, "Woman's Club of Evanston" was stenciled above the entrance to replace the former sign.

While compliance with fire codes had been a concern throughout the 1960s, an updated Evanston Fire Code made the issue more urgent in 1974—at a cost of $38,000. Again, the Club relied on the donations of members, borrowing money from the sinking fund, and a contribution of $5,000 from the Auxiliary. Fire code updates included the installation of a sprinkler system, doors between the first floor foyer and entrance to the tearoom, fire exit lights, and stairway lights, among other renovations. Adding to these costs was the fact that each year something new needed to be fixed—a leaky roof, the furnace—and the décor needed to be kept up-to-date to maintain revenue from rentals. The president appointed a Long Term Planning Committee in December 1960 to study the situation and determine major improvements and renovations to the clubhouse. In addition to donations from members and money from the sinking fund, the Auxiliary often contributed a portion of their Benefit Show proceeds for these ongoing maintenance needs, and in 1971 it donated stage lighting.

Clubhouse maintenance was a major hit to the budget, so proceeds from the annual Antique Show, started in May 1965, went directly to this fund. The May 1966 show netted $4,688 for the Front Entrance Fund. In 1978, the Club raised $5,600, with 185 members working 820 hours on the events. Antique Shows were held at the clubhouse for three days each May from that year on. The show featured dozens of tables of exhibitors selling antiques, along with bake sales and raffles for handmade goods, such as a hand-quilted comforter made by the members. Many of the same exhibitors set up tables year after year and forged relationships with the attendees. Management contracts from 1973–1974 suggest that the Club by that time had hired professional organizers to oversee the Antique Show, but by 1977, the event was so successful that the members decided to manage it themselves rather than seek outside help.

By the 1980s, the Woman's Club of Evanston Charitable Foundation was thriving and able to provide contributions to organizations throughout the local area. As a result, the Club could now afford to put a part of the proceeds of the semiannual Benefit Show back into clubhouse maintenance. Members also continued to donate money out-of-pocket to keep

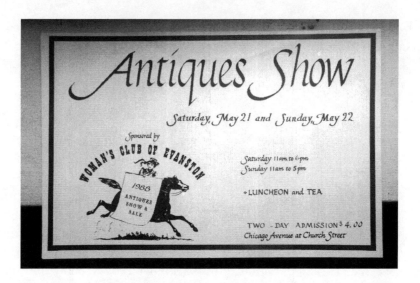

their historic Evanston building alive, up to date, and in safe condition for all to enjoy at meetings, entertainment, wedding ceremonies and receptions, teas and luncheons, and other events. In 1979, the Club received income from seventy rentals, essential revenue as the clubhouse was literally crumbling despite the ongoing repairs. The written history of the first one hundred years of the Club expresses the sense of urgency the members were feeling:

> The previous winter the second floor of the clubhouse
> had been unused for Tuesday programs on the coldest
> days, a symptom of many physical plant problems about to
> demand attention. A large vertical foundation crack in the
> north basement was repaired and deteriorating boiler lines,
> defunct heat exchangers, and sump pumps were replaced.
> Three boilers were reconditioned. By the second year
> (1982), the Club's heating system was working well, and a
> warmer clubhouse encouraged attendance. Concurrently
> it was necessary for the board to grapple with fire escape
> repair, tuckpointing, and plumbing. One bitter-cold day
> the fire-sprinkling water in-take pipes burst, dangerously
> flooding the boiler room. Later a similar problem occurred
> with kitchen pipes. . . .

As the work moved forward the Board of Directors and the House and Grounds Committee dared to become a bit complacent until one day in late July. After a loud cracking noise, the office ceiling began slowly to descend, and, of course, it had to be completely removed and restored. Other damage, caused by heavy floor sanding and the age of the building, soon became apparent. From that day on for the next two years anything that could break, broke.

The Club asked members for extra contributions to the Major Maintenance Fund, and in 1981 alone, 118 members donated $5,687 to the building fund in order to reupholster furnishings and bring the clubhouse up to fire code compliance. In 1984, the Club used donations from members to install a closed-circuit color television in the West Room, which beamed programs to the older members who were unable to climb stairs. In 1986, an archives room was designated to hold all the current and many past Club records, including publicity. Nearly all of the historical records were transferred to Northwestern University in 1991, and the records from 1991 to 2000 (and some beyond) were transferred in 2009. The preservation of these records makes possible research on the history of the Club and the women's club movement in general.

Proving Relevance and Value to the Community

Recently I attended a conference with the leaders of many other suburban women's Clubs. ALL are feeling the financial burden of increased expenses, especially those that maintain Clubhouses and a permanent staff of employees.

But the problem is not only financial. It also involves questions regarding the value and place of women's Clubs in today's world. Federal and local governments are now providing educational classes and welfare programs which used to be sponsored by Clubs like ours. In fact, many of them in our own community were started by this Club.

—Marian Waitley
President, 1963–1965

Throughout its existence, despite the work it has done for the community and beyond, the Woman's Club of Evanston had to prove its importance and relevance to those who did not see the value of its contributions. In the May 1962 *Bulletin,* President Ada Deletzke noted, "It is interesting to recall here that the Woman's Club was instrumental in aiding the forerunner of the present Park Ridge School for Girls which was first located in Evanston. In this connection, we are also reminded that many organizations gained their beginning through Woman's Club efforts, organizations which have long ago gone their independent ways and have forgotten their origins." Throughout the 1960s, the Club worked to adapt to the changing needs of the organizations they had helped. Instead of being discouraged by the notion that their help no longer seemed needed, the members took the self-sustaining nature of these organizations to be a measure of the Club's success. "In reading the history of the Woman's Club," Elizabeth Mueller (President, 1967–1969) explains, "one becomes very conscious of the many projects started by the Club, and then, when self-sustaining, were turned over to the proper authorities. The time is not past for us to continue in this fashion—we must give our support to those community functions and projects which are 'mutually helpful' to all concerned."

The time of social unrest, financial despair, and uncertainty about the Club's future was also marked by conflicts with the city over the Club's properties. The issue of the lot to the north was heating up: the city wanted the land for a parking lot, seeing it as a way to attract more customers to the growing downtown shopping district and generate revenue through parking fees. The Club first leased the land to the city and then finally sold it in 1983 for $283,000.

Beginning in 1959, the Club encountered another conflict with city developers. The Evanston City Council automatically included the Woman's Club in an assessment for lighting on Church Street that would provide for "improvement of retail trade." Paying this assessment would have drawn funds away from clubhouse maintenance, programming, and charity. Further, "shopping center type bright lights detract from the desirability and value of residential property." Not only had the Woman's Club been lumped under the heading of for-profit companies and asked to contribute to this effort, but the proposed lights had the potential to lower property values. After consulting lawyers, the Club learned that fighting this inclusion in the street lighting project would cost far more than the assessment. The lawyers recommended against an appeal, and the Club was forced to drop its case.

In 1976, the Club received notice that it would be taxed unless it could prove that it was "not just a social club," as it had been forced to do in the 1930s when required to pay Social Security tax. The January board minutes read: "A system for recording the number of committee hours expended in the Clubhouse has been devised by the President . . . so that at year's end an accounting of Clubhouse usage will be readily available for tax information purposes." Each chair was required to record her committee or department's hours of service in a book. As the Club's one-hundred-year history noted, "it became a revelation. Everyone who writes in that book on board meeting day is amazed at how those hours mount." It worked, as President Marcia Freeman's report in May 1976 indicates: "We are all concerned with our Tax situation and this December we received notice to appear ten days later before the Court of Appeals covering years '73–'75. I worked diligently preparing an all-inclusive report for our lawyers and the case was dismissed."

The Library Controversy

Ten years later, the Club again became locked in a conflict with government officials, and this time, it would be one of the most expensive and time-consuming fights that they had ever experienced. The Evanston Public Library, located to the west of the clubhouse, wanted to expand and become a 100,000-square-foot facility to meet the needs of its growing population. In January 1987, the library board came up with plans to acquire the Woman's Club property at 615 Church Street, the house just west of the clubhouse, which was being used by young women as a dormitory and as a social center. The acquisition would add 4,000 square feet to the floor plan for the library, and it would also mean moving the alley farther east. Such a move would reduce the Club's viability, as the house that stood there provided the Club with rental income, and it would negatively affect the property value of the clubhouse. The Club was still reeling from its decades-long conflict with the city over turning the property at 1714 Chicago into a parking lot. The clubhouse sat, and still sits as of this writing, on a valuable piece of property in the middle of a constantly evolving retail district. The Club became concerned that if the city acquired both of the two pieces of property surrounding the clubhouse, it might come after the clubhouse itself next.

The Woman's Club argued that the city had not considered all options for the library expansion. Club representatives also pointed out that the city continually mentioned the proposed cost of the library and expressed concern that the expansion would disrupt utility services in the area as well as change the flow of traffic through one of the busiest alleys in Evanston. The Club urged the library to consider other options, such as moving the library to the Northwestern University Research Park, which was being built at the time. Another option the members asked the city to consider involved taking space from the Northwestern University dorms next door. Ann Dienner, head of an ad hoc committee formed to investigate the situation, insisted that the library building had not been well planned in the first place. She wrote, in an opinion piece in October 1988: "It is ironic that in the 1940's the City Council voted to sell off a sizeable lot directly north of the library in order to accommodate the development of the Northwestern Apartments. Thus precluding any future expansion of the library; later, Evanston was left with our present library, popularly considered a major rip-off . . . [the city] expects the Woman's Club to atone for the City's sins of omission, the City's lack of foresight and community concern." The library argued back, stating that all other options had been considered and deemed inappropriate for the building, and that they were being transparent to the citizens of Evanston about the costs. Letters to the editor in the *Evanston Review* contained accusations and opinions from all sides of the issue. The Club's lawyer, Terrence Tysinski, advised that the city could condemn the property at 615 Church, now rented to Evanston residents, and claim eminent domain, since the library is public property. Even though the house had been used to accommodate young working women for several years after World War I, the building had no recognized historical value and could not be designated a landmark and thus made eligible for protection. He indicated that the city had a better case, as they could prove that the library was necessary and that there was no other way to expand. To bring suit against the library could take up to nine months and cost the Club $10,000 to $15,000 in legal fees. The Club approved hiring a public relations professional to enlighten the general public about the Club's purpose and contributions to the community.

It might seem contradictory to the history and aims of the Woman's

Club to argue against the expansion of the library. The Club had worked for decades to increase access to books and education—supporting a traveling library in the early 1900s; sponsoring Library Day at the Club in the 1920s; naming Ida Faye Wright, Evanston librarian and historian, as their second elected honorary member in 1945; holding parties and meetings for the library at the clubhouse; and making the Evanston Public Library a recipient of contributions for decades. Over and over again, the Club asserted that it supported a larger library but wanted more transparent communication about the library's plans. Concerned with much more than just a loss of property and monetary value, the Club worried that its work was not being recognized or valued by the Evanston community. The Club, in other words, was feeling dispensable. Ann Dienner and Amelia Graff expressed this concern in a letter to the Club members: "A proper library is deemed desirable, but as citizens, taxpayers and members, might we not ask . . . at what price? Financially and property wise? Is this prudent, judicious, economically sound planning for Evanston?" Called in to assess the situation, an architect from Hasbrouck Peterson Associates suggested that the Woman's Club maintain the status quo by insisting that its land was not for sale and that the property must be maintained and not disturbed. This would "impose serious design restraints on the new Library facility" but could be accommodated by an architect. However, the architects went on to say, addressing the ad hoc committee:

> The problem with this easy approach is that the Woman's
> Club would be in the awkward position of obstructing the
> expansion of the Library. There seems to be no question of
> the need for expansion and we have been told that there is
> no other likely location for the Library. Were there another
> location which did not affect their property, the Woman's
> Club membership would almost certainly be in the
> forefront of encouraging the expansion. It seems then, that
> finding a previously unconsidered solution to the Library's
> expansion needs is in order.

By March 1988, the city had backed down from the plan to acquire 615 Church, but the issue quickly reemerged. In December, City Manager Joel Asprooth made a monetary offer for the property which the Club rejected. In the meantime, fears that the city would come after the actual clubhouse prompted members to look into acquiring national landmark status for the building. A report from the Mary Knutson of the committee pointed out that this designation would "not prevent a government agency from declaring eminent domain over our property, [but] it would afford us the support and prestige of national and state agencies in our defense. It would also prevent the use of Federal or State funds to be used in conjunction with any project that would involve the demolishing of our building." Although the clubhouse did not attain landmark status until 2006, the difficulties with the city prompted the women to fight for and protect what they still had left—the home base of the Club.

The city proposed a second offer in March 1989, which included $25,000 in cash and a land exchange that would leave the Club with approximately the same square footage and land value. The Club had not responded by May that year, at which point it was facing forced condemnation of the property at 615 Church Street. Ginny Blair (President, 1989–1991) stated: "The Woman's Club must become businesslike and not emotional anymore. Give the city manager a counter proposal with some teeth in it." She later repeated these sentiments, arguing that "that the Woman's Club has shown enough emotionalism and we must get businesslike now and be uncommitted while negotiations are being worked on." The Club made a counter proposal that included a piece of land to the north and compensation to the Club for structural damage, liability damage insurance, loss of utility services, loss of rentals and event/benefit proceeds during construction (due to noise and traffic), loss of rental from 615 Church, assured access for delivery, loss of their mature elm tree, and an appreciation of the property by the city. In October 1989, the city agreed to give the Club $100,000 in compensation and a piece of property on Chicago Avenue north of the clubhouse. Blair explained, "We felt it was only responsible to start acting, rather than reacting," and later stated, "We're entering negotiations with tough counterproposals like responsible citizens, not a bunch of little old biddies."

Five months later, the Club rescinded their counter offer after learning that the land was deemed much more valuable than previously assessed. The Club asked for $200,000 and compensation for the legal fees incurred during the conflict. The city refused and moved toward condemnation. After further negotiation, at a meeting on January 8, 1991, the Club accepted a settlement from the city for the property in the amount of $306,000.

The Woman's Club of Evanston Buildings and Property: A Timeline

1895   Houses stand along the 1700 block of Chicago Avenue and at 615 Church Street.

1910   The Club purchases 1700 Chicago Avenue for the construction of the clubhouse.

1912   The clubhouse is under construction at 1700 Chicago Avenue.

1913   The clubhouse opens in March.

1915   The Club purchases 45 feet of frontage property on Chicago Avenue to extend its grounds north (to 1706 Chicago Avenue). A lawn is seeded, and plans are made for a garden.

1918   The Club purchases 615 Church Street and now owns Lots 11 and 12, as shown on plats from the WCE Archives. The house at 615 Church Street is used for many years by the Girl's League and the Young Woman's Community Club as meeting space and housing for single working girls.

1937   The Club purchases 1714 Chicago Avenue (Lot 13), and the house on the lot is rented as a rooming house. Built in 1854, 1714 Chicago Avenue was home to Evanston's first permanent settlers, John and Hannah Pearsons.

Hannah Pearsons was instrumental in forming the Evanston Educational Aid Association, which supported the education of women at Northwestern University by providing housing and financial aid. The Club's leaders at the time were intentionally creating a buffer between the clubhouse and surrounding development with these land purchases, as downtown Evanston grew.

Property lots (1920) and plat of survey (1960). Credit: Lori Osborne

1938   The house at 1718 Chicago Avenue (Lot 14) is demolished for a city parking lot by the City of Evanston.

1950   A children's playground is put up by the Club on the grounds north of the clubhouse (see "Aiding City's Tiny Children," *Evanston Review*, April 22, 1950, in the WCE Archives).

1972   The Club leases the property at 1714 Chicago Avenue (Lot 13) to the city to expand the parking lot, and the historic house on the lot is torn down. The children's playground was likely removed by this time.

1983   The Club sells 1714 Chicago Avenue to the city for permanent expansion of the parking lot. There is concern among Club members that zoning will permit large structures on the lot.

1990–1991   The property at 615 Church Street is sold to the city for the planned expansion of the public library.

1994   The clubhouse is designated an Evanston landmark.

2006   The clubhouse is listed on the National Register of Historic Places.

The First One Hundred Years

Our Club is a large, vital organization complex in its adminis-
trative structure and dependent upon a supportive membership.
The proof of the success of our cooperative effort has been seen
by all participating in our many calendared activities. Again
we have had an excellent repertoire of enriching programs, we
have enjoyed gracious social functions, we have contributed in
time and money to community projects, we have sought new
members successfully. We have maintained the best of our tra-
ditions while ever striving to improve.

—Doris Overboe
President, 1981–1983

The Club began its centennial celebrations with a luncheon in October 1988, and a week later, the University Guild presented "A Musical Salute to the Woman's Club of Evanston." The Auxiliary presented a program titled "From This Day Forward" on March 2, 1989, one hundred years to the day from the first gathering at Mrs. Harbert's home. The last program of the year featured "A Salute to the Presidents," a slideshow focusing on the fourteen living past presidents. The Centennial Gala was held on April 22, 1989, including dinner and entertainment for members and friends for $50 per ticket. The yearlong celebration recognized the dramatic impact the Club had made, and continued to make, on the community through these decades of alternating hardship and prosperity.

Many women's clubs that arose at the same time as the Woman's Club of Evanston still exist in the greater Chicago area, but a number were forced to close in the latter half of the twentieth century. Like the Woman's Club of Evanston, they experienced falling membership and financial challenges. The Woman's Club of Evanston, however, was determined to survive, refocus its efforts, and draw heavily on the bonds and friendships the women had developed with one other through their common commitment to the community.

Banner commemorating one hundred years of service

What a privilege it has been to serve as President of an organization whose objectives of "mutual helpfulness in all affairs of life, and united effort toward the highest development of humanity" have united and motivated its members through the years and continues to be the rallying cry as we move into the future.

—Ginny Blair
President, 1989–1991

CHAPTER FIVE

Always Forward Thinking, Now Thinking Forward: 1990 to the Present

In the course of the library controversy, community-wide discussion about the Woman's Club of Evanston brought a number of questions to the forefront. City officials and others in the Evanston community thought that the Club was no longer relevant as the needs of the community were being met by other organizations, and many saw the WCE as an affront to the community when it was alleged that the Club was standing in the way of building a library. Some people questioned whether it was wise to continue pouring money into an aging clubhouse and even theorized that women's clubs should go away and leave community work to the "professionals."

But the Club members did not share these doubts. They *were* professionals. Just because women had won the right to vote, could wear pants in public and obtain an education, and were now working outside of the home in record numbers did not mean that women's rights activists should stop advocating for women. And even though social service organizations had been established, they often still needed additional funding and support from organizations such as the Woman's Club of Evanston. The members knew that the community depended on the Club's existence, and they were determined not to give up. These forward-thinking women adapted to the changing times and fought to preserve the Club for its members so that they could continue to be a positive force in the community for generations to come.

Change Happens

WELL—CHANGE HAPPENS! And a good thing it does or
we might still be fighting for the right to vote instead of won-
dering if we made the right life choices. But it occurs to me
that it is only in how we deal with change that really matters.
I figure there are three alternatives: you can wallow in the
past, the "what used to be's" and accomplish nothing but
self-pity; you can fight change with every fiber of your body
and soul, burn yourself and everyone around you out and
again go nowhere; or, you can choose to accept that change
happens, even embrace it, work with it and open yourself up
to endless possibilities.

—Vickie Burke
President, 2000–2001

The Club members knew that change was inevitable. Maintaining the
clubhouse had become increasingly difficult as its members aged along
with its brick foundation and walls. At the same time, the Auxiliary
increased in popularity and energy, putting on a highly successful Benefit
Show each year. By requiring each member to volunteer time in her areas
of interest, the Auxiliary was able to contribute thousands of hours of community service in Evanston.

The saga over land for the library, which ended in 1991, left the Club
stunned. Forced to reenvision their future, the members asked themselves
how they could continue to sustain their presence and work in the community when others viewed the Club's importance as diminishing. At one
time, the Club was the place to be. Public gathering places for women
were scarce in the Club's early years, and women took advantage of the
opportunities it provided as a social milieu and as an outlet for implement-
ing and participating in the reforms that they ardently desired. Ironically,
the Club had succeeded in opening up the public sphere for women,
giving them numerous organizations and spaces in which to participate
professionally and socially with other women—options that meant that
eventually the Club was not the only outlet for the women of Evanston.
Furthermore, the increased mobility of women made it harder to keep
the Club together as one unified organization. Membership retention

became crucial to ensuring that the Club and its beautiful clubhouse in the center of Evanston, remained in place for future generations of women to enjoy its benefits.

As Membership Continues to Decline

I dearly love the Woman's Club building, but even more I love the strength of the wonderfully diverse group of friends I have found within the Woman's Club, both young and old. I would love for you to discover these riches and make it your goal to meet a new friend each time you go to the Clubhouse. This is such a great opportunity to make our Woman's Club an especially unique organization. Let's work together to make it happen!

—Betsy Scherrer
First Vice President, 1999–2000

During the 1970s, membership dropped, and by 1996, the Club had about 250 members. But the Auxiliary remained robust and active, encouraged in part by the ever-widening age range that made up its membership. The Auxiliary's upper limit jumped from age forty-one in 1987 to forty-five by 1996. In 1994, more than half of the members had joined within the past year, leading to concerns that the group might lack a cohesive perspective. The increase in new members brought new challenges for the Auxiliary: at a 1994 board meeting, it was noted that many women expressed difficulty in making friends in the organization and that the nature of the Auxiliary's many projects, which revolved around community service, prevented them from getting to know each other on a more personal level. In response, the Auxiliary added more social and evening events.

In 1996, the members formed an All-Auxiliary Community Service Project Committee to explore and "deliver to the North Shore Community an end product which enhanced everyone's sense of community, celebrated the cultural, ethnic, economic, and intellectual diversity of the community, tapped into the intergenerational strength of the Woman's Club, and highlighted the contributions of the organizations and individuals who laid the groundwork for the successful culture we are proud to be a part of today." Growing membership brought great joy and new skills to the Auxiliary but required the members to rethink their strategies for retention to keep the momentum going.

The Auxiliary also paid careful attention to the scheduling of events. In prior decades, they experimented with meetings and volunteer activities held in the evening and dinners instead of lunches, which seemed to be popular. Much discussion in the board minutes and memos indicate that the board recognized that burnout was a distinct possibility if the calendar was too full and large events were too close together. For example, a memo from Loreen Mershimer dated July 17, 1996, reads, "Right now we have approximately 350–375 project spots [volunteer shifts] for fall, which always runs higher than spring due to Fairy Tale Trail and Merry Merry Market. . . . We could move some of the projects to spring. . . . We could try to reduce the number of slots for some projects." Tension regarding scheduling was reflected in the numerous mentions of babysitting for meetings and events and adaptation to children's schedules. The archives room was used for babysitting, and local sitters were hired to watch members' children.

In addition to scheduling events and meetings around the needs of children, the Auxiliary also included children and husbands in activities. Family parties, ice cream socials, and children's fashion shows dotted the calendar each year, reflecting the members' commitment to family first. By exposing children to Club life, the women saw an opportunity to instill in this next generation an interest in community service. As Donna Brown (Auxiliary President, 1990–1991) recalls:

> My memories of my own daughters heading up to the
> third floor with lunch buckets in hand while I ran or
> attended luncheons and programs also brought memories
> of them on the back porch one summer playing "Woman's
> Club" instead of the standard "school." . . .Listening to
> them repeat some of our discussions was a good lesson for
> me in that young children hear things even when they
> supposedly aren't paying any attention. Naturally, my hope
> is that someday early in the next century they will find
> their way back here as prospective members.

Becoming One

The Woman's Club and the Auxiliary continued to diverge, with one appearing to thrive and the other to fizzle. The Woman's Club had difficulty getting any press in the *Evanston Review* save for a few pictures and brief announcements of events, while the Auxiliary received regular columns and a full cover for their annual Benefit Show. Club and Auxiliary interests clashed in the mid-1990s over Auxiliary dues and use of the clubhouse. In 1992–1993, the two parts of the organization agreed that the Auxiliary would pay a flat fee of $8,000 a year rather than submitting piecemeal payments for dues, insurance, and maintenance for each event. With decreasing rentals and membership, the Woman's Club was coming to the realization that it would not survive unless it reached out to this widening, increasingly diverse group of women. In 1993, the organizations created a "graduate" membership status: "Any person who has elected to graduate from active or inactive membership from the Auxiliary may become a Graduate Member" of the Woman's Club. Graduate members paid lower dues and had less responsibility but still remained associated with the Club. This category was created to encourage continued membership, thereby raising more money for the increasing costs of clubhouse maintenance.

But by 1995, the Club had eliminated the graduate membership status, and all graduates of the Auxiliary could choose to become either active or associate members of the Club. Some members had expressed interest in staying in the Auxiliary, which was one reason for bumping up the age limit; they did not want to move up because they were not interested in doing the work that the WCE was doing or they simply preferred the projects and activities of the Auxiliary. Also in 1995, the Club charged the Auxiliary's Woman's Club relations officer with all the scheduling and coordinating of the entire Club calendar, which was a very meaningful step for the Club to take. By opening its doors to the younger branch, the Club was admitting that the members could no longer handle the pressures of running this organization. In 1996, due to "the value of the Auxiliary members, their enthusiasm and their helpfulness," particularly in achieving ADA compliance for the clubhouse, the board, according to its June 11 meeting minutes, proposed an addition to the standing rules that "an Auxiliary member shall have such privileges and responsibilities as the Board of Directors may grant, including but not limited to serving on committees." The Club and its Auxiliary grew closer together as one organization. The Auxiliary had been started after young women had proven their worthiness in time of war; this time, they had proven themselves resilient and resourceful through years of much smaller hardships in the Club. The Club needed their youth, strength, and help, and it was willing to adapt to include this new generation.

A joint committee on "Planning for the Second Century" (composed of five members each from the Club and the Auxiliary, with a focus on planning for the year 2000) and the Long Range Planning Committee worked together for several months to address the needs of both groups, concluding in January 1996 that "the changing nature of our membership, the substantial financial needs of our Clubhouse and the blurring of the age barrier between the two groups have all led us to the inevitable conclusion that, in a few years, our organization should be one, healthy, unified group. . . . We believe that the emergent organization will be strong, vibrant and will reflect the best points of both groups." They indicated a month later that the Club and clubhouse depended on the forces of both of these groups:

> Our property is a valuable piece of real estate, one in which
> the City of Evanston has an interest. We must continue
> to maintain our Clubhouse and fulfill our purpose as
> an organization in order to assure our future. . . . The
> decreasing and aging membership of the active Woman's
> Club members could result in the inability to carry on
> the responsibilities of the Club. The long-term financial
> stability of the Club becomes tenuous with dwindling
> members. Rentals provide us with much needed operating
> funds, but members and their dues are still needed to keep
> the Club functioning.

As a result, the committees finally proposed a streamlined merger of the Woman's Club and the Auxiliary at a board meeting in January 1997. After the members approved the measure, the women got to work on the transition. Starting in the 1997–1998 Club year, women had the option of being dual members in both organizations until the merger. Members of both groups made up the 1998–1999 nominating committee and were charged with choosing the first combined Board of Directors to be elected in January 1999. A memo dated October 15, 1998, reads: "Obviously, this first merged Board needs to be a strong one as we move into what is going to be a wonderful mix of the familiar and the new. Experienced Board members will help bring stability to the transition. Please consider being part of this Board that will lead The Woman's Club of Evanston into a new chapter of its history." These two transitional years were spent educating members, rewriting bylaws and Club policies, and reassessing community service and philanthropic projects.

With the Auxiliary joining forces with the organization that was responsible for its existence, the two groups sought to "continue to offer a place for our sisters and daughters to experience volunteerism through personal growth and support while also allowing our mothers and grandmothers to continue to remain active without the enormous responsibilities that are a natural part of running this Club." "We are experiencing an *ending*, a *beginning*, and a *continuance!*" exclaimed Vickie Burke (President, 2000–2001). Sara Brenner, the Auxiliary's last president before the merger (1998–1999), at the May 1999 annual Auxiliary luncheon said: "I believe as Auxiliary members we have so much in common with you, and there's so much we can offer one another. I am convinced our merged organization will benefit all of us enormously and will preserve what we all value most about each of our unique structures. There may be a few bumps along the way during these transition years, but I truly believe the 'new' Woman's Club of Evanston will be stronger than ever." The merging of the two organizations promoted connections and relationships across generations, ensuring the Club's sustainability in the community for years to come. It also opened up the Club to greater diversity, promoting a more welcoming atmosphere for prospective members of all ages, races, and marital statuses.

Greater diversity exposed members to new ideas, service opportunities, and more, but it also made it more difficult to meet the unique needs of each individual member. An announcement about the first combined annual meeting in May 2000—which was not a lunch, as the Club had always held, or a dinner, as had been the Auxiliary's tradition, but instead a weekday brunch—read: "Please come. We recognize that this will be difficult for working members. We struggled with scheduling of this event and we know we are bold to suggest that you take the morning off. However, this is the most important meeting of the year. Being part of the 'business' of the Club and exercising our privilege to vote can only strengthen our connection to this organization and our fellow members." Vickie Burke reminded them in the 2001 *Bulletin* to keep trying: "With time, commitment and patience, we will continue to grow together in positive and exciting ways. We are The Woman's Club of Evanston and should be very proud indeed."

The Club continued to make its members feel welcome. The Hospitality Committee remained active, working to make sure that everyone who walked through the clubhouse doors was greeted with a smile. The long-standing Membership Committee took over these welcoming duties, realizing the importance of making both prospective and current members feel at home. It has put on frequent and regular new member teas, luncheons, and dessert socials, established nametag policies, created new member tables at social events, and done much to foster a sense of togetherness for both new and well-established members. Yet the Club had realized in its most recent decades that it is not enough to sit by and wait for women to come to them. Instead, the Club needed to reach out continually and be proactive in forming connections, educating the public on their purpose, and opening its doors to an even wider array of women. The *Bulletin* of September 2001 read, "This year we are trying to accommodate the many interests of Club members by holding Tuesday programs, some evening programs, and a variety of programs that you, our members, have requested."

Several initiatives to encourage membership were proposed during the 1990s: providing a reward or stimulus when members brought in new members, encouraging members to bring friends to meetings and programs, setting up information booths at Evanston events, and leaving informative brochures at public buildings around Evanston. The Club had always had different membership levels, and now it experimented with a number of new levels to meet members on *their* level and respect the many different stages members were at in their lives. The Auxiliary had created an inactive member status before the merger, which exempted members from having to meet the full community service requirement for a period of up to one year at a time while keeping them socially connected. This allowed women to remain connected to the Club during times when they also had to deal with major life events such as having children, changing careers, and the like. Harkening back to its original principle of "unity in diversity," the Club realized that it must recognize the diverse needs of its members if it wanted to remain relevant and strong.

Most significantly, the Club loosened its membership requirements. Since its inception, Club membership depended on who you knew and which social circles you moved in. Prospective members had to be nominated by an established member and voted on by the board after submitting one's qualifications and proving one's worth to the community. This requirement was designed to ensure a membership made up of determined women who would carry out plans to improve the community, and it seems to have worked fine in earlier times, when families did not move around as much and generation after generation remained in the same community. As American society became more mobile, new families regularly moved to and from Evanston, reshaping the community and dismantling the networks that had been built up over decades. Many women were coming into the Evanston community without a single connection, which led the Club to shift its membership focus in the late 1990s to who the prospective member was as an individual rather than who she knew.

Before the merger, the Auxiliary began a series of Prospective Member Workshops for those going through the membership process. This allowed prospective and established members a chance to get to know each other before a commitment was made. During this trial period, prospective members not only attended several workshops, they participated in a certain number of community service activities and attended committee meetings, social functions, and programs. The Auxiliary assigned a sponsor to each prospective member, and the sponsor advised the Membership chair when the prospective member had completed the requirements. If two-thirds of the board voted to accept the candidate, she became a member. In the early years, the Club had required a unanimous vote on new members, but gradually it began to loosen that requirement. These more open membership practices paid off: ninety-seven women joined (new and reinstated) between 1998 and 1999. The membership numbered 513 by May 2000, which was after the merger. Increased membership, however, also generated increased operating costs, making it necessary to increase dues to $100 in 2001 and to $135 in 2008.

After the merger, the Club made other changes. The president's term was reduced to one year to reflect what the Auxiliary had been doing since 1983. To ensure more efficient operations and communications, the Club set about to streamline its processes and embrace new technologies. In March 1993, a letter to the Auxiliary noted: "we need to determine once and for all if we are buying a computer and who will be responsible for it." That same year, the Auxiliary spent nearly $3,000 on a computer and printer, the typical cost for this new technology at the time.

New technology ushered in new channels to communicate to members. Although the *Bulletin*, published monthly since 1911, imposed a great expense, the Club needed it to communicate and keep the members connected. In the earliest days of the Club, Nellie Kingsley recalls tramping "from one end of the town to the other because I was corresponding secretary. It seems to me that I did nothing else that year but address postal cards, because in those days we didn't have the money that we have now, and the cards all had to be written, and it was some job to write out two or three hundred. The work seemed stupendous."

Today, communications are much easier and nearly instantaneous with cell phones, the Internet and with nearly all members now owning computers and other devices to keep them connected. Reflecting this rapidly changing technology, Jane DeMoss (President, 2005–2006) observed that "to improve our overall communication with members, we used blast email, the *Bulletin* and Club website, www.wcofe.org." New communication technologies reduced printing needs and helped to lower costs. In 2009, the *Bulletin* reported that 75 percent of the members had opted to "go green" by electing to receiving the monthly newsletter electronically.

As valuable as these rapidly improving communication technologies have been to the Club, they have also presented challenges in using them effectively. In 2009, President Julie Chernoff created an IT Strategy Committee to examine and address the Club's technology needs moving forward. In addition, the Communications Committee works to ensure that the Club is presenting thorough, transparent, correct, and relevant information in a timely manner to members and the general public.

Communications glitches have caused concern throughout the Club's history. On occasion, press releases and articles have gone to publication without approval by the appropriate committee, event information has reached those in charge of publicity too late, and incorrect information has been conveyed to the public. Today's communication technologies face the same challenges, but the proliferation of information outlets and the ease with which information can be distributed have made communication even more difficult to control.

Reflecting Our Community

In an effort to expand the Club's membership to better reflect the diversity of women in Evanston and ensure that the organization serve as a resource for all women, the Club created the Inclusion and Diversity Exploration Task Force in 2010. Its mission was to examine the Club's diversity profile past and present, explore "our image, role, peers and partners in our wider community," and develop a plan for "a 21st century Woman's Club of Evanston that reflects and supports all women across our community." A 2011 membership survey (253 respondents) and a 2012 Perceptions of Diversity survey (50 respondents) revealed that the Club was made up primarily of white, married, college-educated women between the ages of forty-five and sixty-five, who were liberal on social issues and had an income of at least $100,000. Overwhelmingly, these members expressed a desire and need to increase diversity in the Club. In response, the Club held a World Café to promote "an open and creative conversation on a topic of mutual interest." The purpose of the event was to gather a group of members to pool their collective knowledge, share ideas and insights, and gain a deeper understanding of the subject and issues involved. Similar to the Open Forums that the Club held after World War I, the café provided an informal setting where women discussed what they felt were pressing issues of the time. The results from the diversity and inclusion study and corresponding World Café would be used to inform club policy and development in the years that followed.

How to Maintain Our Home

In many ways, the clubhouse has been the glue that has held the Club together. Unlike many other women's clubs that have not been able to overcome the rising costs of an aging clubhouse, the Evanston clubhouse has stood strong, thanks to careful planning and the support of its members and the community. At the 1997 annual meeting, Doris Overboe (President, 1981–1983) gave a history of clubhouse maintenance, explaining that it was "noise, mess, dust . . . but it was progress!" The clubhouse would not be what it is today without the work also of many determined paid employees, and the Club looked after the personal needs of those individuals who took care of the clubhouse. When Ores Jackson, who had been the Club's custodian and maintenance worker since 1957, was injured in a hit-and-run accident in 1990, the Club collaborated with other Evanston organizations to raise thousands of dollars to defray his medical costs.

The joys of homeownership always come with hardships. Since the clubhouse first opened in 1913, the Club has made improvements, upgrades, and much needed repairs every year. From landscaping in the first years, to adding a kitchen and widening the driveway, to repairing the foundation and dealing with leaks, to continual reupholstering, rewiring, and refinishing, and everything in between, the women have addressed the problems as they have come up, constantly seeking new ways to raise funds for maintenance while still being able to contribute as much money to the community as possible. The Auxiliary contributed funds from its own revenue, especially after the Benefit Show moved back to the clubhouse in 1988. (The show had been moved in 1974, when it was deemed unsafe to use the lighting equipment.) The Auxiliary's $30,000 Save the Stage campaign in 1988 paid for rewiring the auditorium, new curtains, and much more. In 2001, the Club installed air conditioning, adding to the comfort of members, their guests, and the many groups who rented event space in the clubhouse throughout the year.

ADA Compliance

A growing awareness of, and sensitivity to, the needs of individuals with disabilities led to the passage of the Americans with Disabilities Act in 1990. The clubhouse being some eighty years old, accessibility accommodations had not been built into its structure, and the Club discovered that it was going to be prohibitively expensive to integrate these features. A suit brought against the Club in 1994 forced them to acknowledge that legally it had to move forward with providing these accommodations. The Club examined its finances, hired lawyers and consultants, and created the Get a Lift (GAL) campaign to raise funds to provide full access to the first and second floors. The GAL fund helped minimize the impact that these modifications would have made on the Club's income and operating expenses.

The consultants' recommendations, which took into account both cosmetic considerations and ease of use, brought the cost to $150,000. Because the clubhouse had been designated a historic building by the Evanston Preservation Commission, the Club faced costly challenges in making modifications that would not disrupt the structural, aesthetic, and historic integrity of the building. The board decided to install an elevator between the basement, first, and second floors, place a ramp at the front of the clubhouse, and renovate the bathrooms. These modifications to make the building ADA compliant added another $50,000 to the original cost. A letter to the members dated January 31, 1997, indicates that the Club's funding efforts had fallen short of the needed $150,000, and they agreed to access the Investment Management Account (IMA) that had been created when a member bequeathed $160,000 to the Club. Eventually the financial picture was resolved, and the elevator, ramps, and renovated bathrooms were ready in late September 1997, making the Club fully accessible to all members and guests.

The Capital Campaign: This Old House, Part II

After making the expenditures to meet ADA compliance, the Club faced the dual problems of an ever-aging clubhouse and decreased rental income. Realizing that much work had to be done, in 2003 the Club hired the architectural firm of Rodie/Scherrer, Inc., to assess the property. Their assessments revealed the need for $820,000 worth of repairs, including new boilers ($300,000); exterior painting; masonry, roof, and gutter repairs ($300,000); fire alarm and sprinkler system upgrades; landscaping and exterior improvements; and art and archival preservation and renovation of the archives room. Numerous smaller repairs and upgrades also needed to be made around the clubhouse, as determined by the members. In October 2003 Wendy Irwin suggested to the Finance Committee that the Club embark on a major capital campaign. With the clubhouse long overdue for these major repairs, the Club decided to make this a priority for the next couple of years. Plans came to fruition in 2005, when

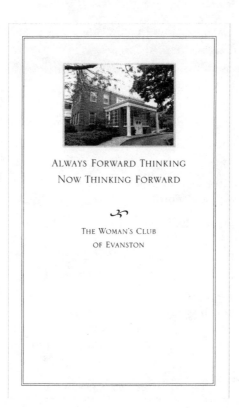

ALWAYS FORWARD THINKING
NOW THINKING FORWARD

THE WOMAN'S CLUB
OF EVANSTON

Cover of the Capital Campaign brochure, 2005
CREDIT: CAPITAL CAMPAIGN COMMITTEE

campaign manager Wendy Irwin and co-chairs Vickie Burke and Diane Golan worked through the summer to roll out the capital campaign at the President's Dinner on September 20. With a goal of 100 percent Club member participation and $1 million dollars, the women were in for a very difficult time.

The support of the membership and the community quickly became apparent. Within two months of announcing the start of the campaign, the Club had received over $780,000 in pledges, which could be paid in installments over a period of five years. In the November 2005 *Bulletin*, Wendy Irwin commented: "Typical of the members of this organization, your support of the campaign is nothing short of spectacular." Terry Dason (President, 2007–2008) explained that "the Club members were carefully solicited in a variety of ways to encourage their generosity without overreaching or expecting too little." Each woman gave as she could. Three prominent local businesses also contributed a total of $75,000. By November 2006, the Club had raised $932,000, and it reached its goal of $1 million by the spring of 2008, with nearly all of it collected by 2010. The first major renovation undertaken was to entirely replace the roof in 2006.

At the conclusion of the capital campaign, an ad hoc committee called the Capital Campaign Fund Expenditure Committee (CCFEC) was formed to manage the remaining campaign funds and to ensure that the campaign promises made to the donors were upheld.

These improvements have made the clubhouse a sought-after space for events by organizations and individuals throughout the Chicago area,

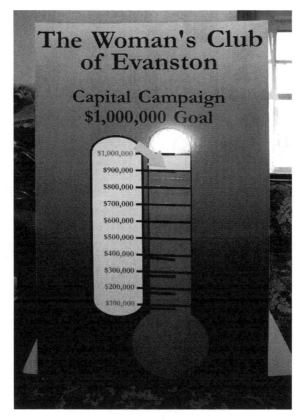

On our way to our $1,000,000 goal
CREDIT: CAPITAL CAMPAIGN COMMITTEE

including weddings, meetings, benefits, performances, and productions. At one time, the Club relied on word-of-mouth recommendations; today, those looking for an event space can find reviews online—and for the clubhouse they see rave reviews, especially from those who have held weddings there.

During the capital campaign, the women celebrated another milestone in the preservation of the clubhouse. In 2006, after much historical research, writing, and planning, the clubhouse was listed on the National Register of Historic Places. A property achieves this designation only after analysis and a recommendation by a state advisory board and final approval by the Secretary of the Interior. National Register status is given only to properties of exceptional historical significance, and once attained, anyone doing work in the area of the property (utilities, for example, or building construction) must give special consideration and protection to the preservation of the property. The clubhouse had already been designated an Evanston Landmark in 1994 by the Evanston Preservation Commission, which afforded some protection. Having national status created another layer of security protecting the Club's property and assets.

Programming for the Modern Woman

In the 1990s and the first decades of the new century, the Club continued its educational programming in line with its commitment to "mutual self-improvement." A majority of the women who were members had completed advanced degrees and held leadership positions in the workforce, and these programs were designed to enhance and complement their knowledge and to keep them up to date on the latest trends in every field. As had always been the practice, the Club invited leading-edge artists, politicians, reporters, authors, physicians, scientists, and others to discuss their work. Programming remained diverse; for example, in 2007–2008, both the Tuesday and Friday programs included wine tasting and cheese making, purchasing and preparing local produce, holiday gift ideas, talks by curators from the Art Institute of Chicago and the Field Museum discussing current exhibits, author talks and book discussions, antiques appraisal, and theater. In November 1990, news anchor Bill Kurtis gave a talk about the destruction of rain forests; in 2000, the women heard a travelogue about China.

Field trips continued to be popular. In recent years, the women have toured the Mitchell Museum of the American Indian, the Botanic Gardens, the Field Museum, and the National Broadcast Museum, among other cultural venues. Inviting a diverse array of people—from the Evanston community, the Chicago area, and beyond—to speak on the most current topics of interest allowed the women opportunities to enhance their knowledge, meet new people, and socialize while enriching their minds.

Reaffirming Our Community Value

The library and parking lot controversies opened the members' eyes to the fact that the Club was not an isolated organization. Yet, not everyone recognized its value in the community, and even as extensive repairs and major funding were being put toward preserving the clubhouse, the cracks in the Club's relationship with the surrounding community were growing larger as time went on. With their reputation on the line, the Club was not about to lose the building that had housed so many memories and so many thousands of hours of hard work. To guard against this possibility, the women reached out and established connections with the movers and shakers of Evanston. They joined the Chamber of Commerce in the late 1980s, which enabled members to attend meetings and have their voices heard, particularly on matters of the central business district, where the clubhouse was located. In December 1993, the Club hosted a Chamber of Commerce Business After Hours holiday gathering with all proceeds going to the Evanston Shelter for Battered Women. Some of the Chamber of Commerce monthly meetings were also held at the clubhouse. In 1994, then mayor Lorraine Morton called a meeting of religious leaders at the clubhouse to discover better ways to communicate and work together on city matters. A Civics Committee, closely mirroring the many manifestations of the Club's earlier civics committees, was reinvigorated to examine city planning initiatives as they arose. The value of the Club was no longer assumed; the women had to work for it. And work they did.

Our Unbroken Thread of Giving

So where do we take the WCE in its second hundred years of activity? How do we maintain our community-mindedness in an age filled with such poverty, prosperity, anxiety, can-do spirit, appalling ignorance and deep springs of compassion? How do we increase our impact on our town and region, and continue to attract the most talented, interesting, and hardworking women around?. . . Whatever future we create, we will do it together, with our sisters of the past to inspire us.

—Patty Shaw Sprague
President, 2006–2007

The Club's commitment to community service has remained focused on the needs of women and children. Organizations and agencies with greater resources for meeting the needs of the community have been established, but the Club continues to be a stabilizing force, filling in the cracks and gaps with additional funding and the personal touch that supports those in need. Club members' educational and professional backgrounds have provided the skill to raise money throughout its history, but their roles as wives, sisters, aunts, daughters, and mothers have given them the ability to see where individual, personal care is beneficial.

Time and Talent

Throughout the 1980s and 1990s, and before the merger with the Young Woman's Auxiliary, the Woman's Club focused on a few community service projects, including Evanston Meals at Home, Evanston Hospital volunteers, welfare sewing and knitting, and a senior citizens volunteer recognition tea at the Levy Center in Evanston. The Club also continued its annual spring benefit, which generally included dinner and a fashion show. The Auxiliary, however, had a continually changing schedule of community service projects for members to pursue. Each month, the newsletter announced several different projects in which to participate — some completely different from month to month — with a variety of projects to appeal to members' diverse interests and busy schedules. Many YWA members were newlyweds and/or had demanding careers, and many had young children at home. Donna Brown (Auxiliary President, 1990–1991), speaking at the 1998 President's Dinner, explained: "The flexibility of the projects offered have always been perfect for women either at home or in the paid workforce." At the 1999 annual luncheon, Sara Brenner summarized the group's activities:

> The Auxiliary gave over two thousand hours of service
> to about twenty agencies throughout Evanston and the
> surrounding communities. We continued to support
> our favorites like Evanston Meals at Home, the First
> Presbyterian Soup Kitchen, and KEB Trashbusters. We
> caroled at local nursing homes and baked goodies for
> various area shelters. We planted gardens and had one-on-
> one craft time at the Rice Children's Home, and painted
> rooms at the YWCA Battered Woman's Shelter. Our
> biggest community service project, the Fairy Tale Trail, was
> once again held at our fully accessible clubhouse.

The Auxiliary truly had something for everyone.

The Auxiliary's strict community service requirement for active membership made it essential for members to fit in these service activities. According to the Auxiliary handbook, published in 1995: "Each member must share in the work of her chosen committee; each member must participate in at least three community service projects; each member must participate in one aspect of the Benefit Show; each member must be financially responsible for the sale of at least two adult tickets to the Benefit Show." Being a part of this network did not depend on how much money you had, where you lived, what your educational background was, or who your parents were, but it did depend on being a strong, determined woman ready to make her community a better place for her own children and all others.

While many community service activities were diverse, changing to reflect the interests of members, some were long-standing, including the Bake-A-Night to benefit a variety of organizations in Evanston, the First Presbyterian Soup Kitchen, Evanston Meals at Home, and numerous toy, diaper, formula, and clothing drives. The Hours Book, established many years before, was still passed around at meetings to record this activity.

One of the Club's longest-standing community outreach projects remains the toy drives—from the first documented event in 1890, which ensured every child in Evanston would have a Christmas present, to recent holiday toy collections for children and families through Family Focus. The Club has also held book donation drives called Reach Out and Read to collect books for the Children and Adolescent Clinic at Evanston Hospital.

Treasure

Extensive fundraising complements hands-on community service and volunteering. Before the merger, the Auxiliary created its own foundation analogous to the Woman's Club's Charitable Foundation. This 501(c)(3) organization allowed the Auxiliary to raise charitable funds without paying Illinois state sales tax. Like the Charitable Foundation, its purposes were "to promote and advance educational, charitable, civic, health and welfare activities and support and assist organizations dedicated to those purposes." According to the Auxiliary's 1995 handbook, this fund was made up of proceeds from ad book sales, the Benefit Show, Merry Merry Market, and the benefit dinner dance; funds were distributed to local charities and also used to create the Fairy Tale Trail, a hands-on, fully accessible Halloween activity for kids with special needs. The Auxiliary's operating account took in funds from various activities, such as raffles, T-shirt sales, and bake sales, as well as membership dues. Operating expenses included the needs of board members, cost of printing the newsletter and "green books" (the annual yearbook, which functioned as a directory), and clubhouse use (with a portion of the dues going to the Woman's Club of Evanston). The Auxiliary also used a portion of its operating budget to provide scholarships for graduating Evanston Township High School students bound for college.

The Auxiliary held its first Benefit Show in 1951, and the event became increasingly popular throughout the 1980s and 1990s. The Woman's Club held its own benefit fashion shows and parties, but after the merger the Auxiliary's Benefit Show became the primary fundraising event of the year. "Although the Show has taken on many forms since its inception," the Auxiliary 1995 handbook states, "today it revolves around a central theme with a mix of characters and musical vignettes. Participation in

Merry Merry Market memorabilia

Cornucopia poster, 2013

the show itself is open to all Auxiliary members and their families. The motto of 'No Talent Required' always prevails but never shows." The Auxiliary required all active members to be involved in at least one aspect of this annual event: acting, producing, script writing and reading, or selling ads for the ad book. Both the Club and the Auxiliary continued to hold annual dinner dances, but these events were adjusted to fit the changing philanthropic landscape. From 1973 to 1990, the Auxiliary renamed its annual benefit dinner dance "Benefit Backers" to encourage sponsorship. Giving "Backer" status to donors, the Auxiliary raised funds through ticket sales, corporate donations, and a silent auction. Reflecting the increase of women in the workforce, a newsletter advertisement encouraged members to ask "the company that you (or your husband) work for" to become a sponsor. During the 1990s, to encourage increased donations from corporations and the public, the Auxiliary began to focus its two large fundraising events on a single charity, a practice the Club had adopted in the 1980s. Continuing this tradition today, the Club designates one beneficiary for the annual Benefit Show and another for the annual benefit dinner dance. Additional smaller contributions raised during events throughout the year go to a variety of other charitable organizations, which are then listed in every Benefit Show ad book.

Of all the Auxiliary's fundraising events throughout the year none was more successful than Merry Merry Market. This annual November event featured fifty to seventy local artisans selling their wares in time for the Christmas season, and for several years, Merry Merry Market also featured a tree and plant sale, boosting the Auxiliary's proceeds. The Auxiliary distributed proceeds from ticket sales to a variety of charities in the northern and northwestern Chicago suburbs. Begun in 1987, it was attracting more than two thousand visitors per year and raising over $10,000 annually by 1995. It was even featured on the *Today Show*. One popular feature of the market was the Sugar Plum Shop, which helped children create items to proudly give to their families at Christmas. In 2002, the Club changed the market's name to Cornucopia. That year, the November newsletter described Cornucopia as a "Holiday Harvest of Gifts," with a juried arts and crafts fair. Today it is known as the Holiday Bazaar.

The Auxiliary generally stipulated that contributions be earmarked for a particular need rather than for general operation expenses, a practice that continues today. The Club supports organizations through which it can make the most profound impact on the community and stretch its financial and volunteer contributions the furthest. Club members contribute hours and hours of work each year, and the Club earmarks benefit proceeds and donations for organizations that do not receive sufficient outside funding or that need help in starting a particular worthwhile service.

Healthy Communities

In the last twenty-five years, the Club has provided thousands of hours of service and hundreds of thousands of dollars in contributions to a number of health organizations in Evanston and the greater North Shore area. In response to the spread of HIV/AIDS throughout the 1980s and 1990s, the Club provided support to BE-HIV, a program designed to provide support groups, counseling, domestic assistance, case management, risk reduction, and education to those with or at risk for HIV/AIDS in the north and northwest suburbs. This organization was the recipient of proceeds from the first spring benefit dinner dance after the merger in 2000. BE-HIV also benefited, along with PAWS Animal Shelter and Howard Brown Women's Programs, from the Proud to Run race, which the Club helped to staff. The Club also supported Women and Children HIV Positive, a program at Cook County Hospital that provided medical and psychosocial services to women and children affected by HIV/AIDS, and gave over $2,000 to its art/play therapy program for children in 1991–1992.

When the flu vaccine was invented, the Club and Auxiliary began leading efforts to make it accessible. In 1996, a flu shot clinic was held at the clubhouse. "If you can't afford to catch the flu this season," a letter to members read, "it's worth a shot from the Visiting Nurse Association North!" A century after it paid the first year's salary of Fannie Faltz, Evanston's first visiting nurse, in 1897, the Club was still collaborating with the organization it had helped to found. Throughout the decades, the Visiting Nurse Association and the NorthShore Hospice Care (an outgrowth of the association) were the designated recipients of various Club benefit events. In the 1990s, the organization was working to eradicate the flu virus. In 1993, the Visiting Nurse Association recognized the Club at its ninety-fifth anniversary celebration and presented a framed tribute to the Club. The Club continued to sew garments for the Visiting Nurses until it was incorporated into Evanston Northwestern Health Home Services in 1997.

Another project involved breast cancer awareness and as knowledge about it increased throughout the country, the Club began to educate its members about this disease. In 1993, the Auxiliary organized a Breast Cancer Awareness program and also participated in the American Cancer Society's Tell-a-Friend program, in which women called friends and acquaintances, reminded them to make an appointment for a mammogram, and then followed up afterward. This networking not only encouraged physical health but also provided emotional support.

As teen pregnancy and sexual and emotional health became more prominent concerns, the Club and Auxiliary supported efforts to provide services to those in need. In more recent years, the Club provided funds to the Autism Society of Illinois, the Epilepsy Foundation, the Multiple Sclerosis Society, and others, directing funding to the areas where the members felt they could have the most impact.

The Woman's Club gave $3,600 to help start the first hospital in Evanston, and today the Club continues to contribute to the creation of programs at hospitals in Evanston and Chicago. In 1997, the Auxiliary gave $27,000 to build and furnish a room for the Cook County Pediatric Oncology Therapy program. Other recipients include Evanston Northwestern Healthcare's Cancer Research and the Palliative Care Center of the North Shore. The members also use the clubhouse as an extension of the hospital to conduct blood drives, as they had for decades, especially during times of war.

Dressing for Success

Club members volunteer at Deacon's Closet, a resale clothing shop at the First Presbyterian Church in Evanston, staffing the shop, sorting clothing, and donating goods. The Club has also supported the Evanston School Children's Clothing Association, which distributes articles of clothing, mainly for the winter, to children and families in need.

In 2005, the Club launched one of its most popular projects, the Dreams Delivered Prom Boutique, which provides dresses, shoes, jewelry, and accessories to Evanston Township High School students each year for prom. The June/July 2008 *Bulletin* noted, "Girls beamed and their moms cried when denim was traded for lace and each girl transformed into a princess. Our success was confirmed the next day as thank you notes

Dreams Delivered Prom Boutique

arrived from the girls in the form of text messages!" The Club collects new and gently used dresses, shoes, and accessories to be given to the girls. The community comes together to help. Kenny the Kleener provides dry cleaning free of charge. In 2012, the Ivy Pearl Foundation, the Delta Chi chapter of the Alpha Kappa Alpha sorority, and Pivot Point Academy donated time and services to help with hair and makeup. Dreams Delivered is currently one of the recipients of proceeds from Central Street Spring Community Day, sponsored by participating businesses on Central Street.

Throughout the 1980s and 1990s, with financial help from the Woman's Club of Evanston Charitable Foundation, the sewing group created complete infant layette sets to be distributed to the Evanston Health Department. According to a letter from Karen A. Seals, Division Chief for Personal Health Services, Evanston Health Department, to Doris Anderson, WCE President, dated December 3, 1997, it was a project that became a holiday tradition that the health department "truly look[ed] forward to." Welfare Sewing, the Club's longest-standing continual volunteer activity,

Welfare sewing, late 1990s

continues to this day, gathering monthly to use the sewing machines that were purchased in 1925. In recent years, it has taken on new projects. For the American Cancer Society of Evanston, the group created colorful comfort pillows for breast cancer patients and breast forms for women to use before they undergo reconstructive surgery. Members have sewn adaptive clothing for men and women who served in Iraq, contributed through the organization Sew Much Comfort. They also provide sewing for the Club's Benefit Show, Fairy Tale Trail, and Dreams Delivered Prom Boutique. In 2014, the committee changed its name to the Sewing Circle to reflect a more inclusive environment and the circle of friendship among the committee members.

Nourishing the Body

In recent decades, both the Club and Auxiliary members have contributed hours and dollars to Evanston Meals at Home, spending several days a week preparing and delivering nourishing meals to individuals unable to leave home. On Bake-A-Nights at the clubhouse, members (and sometimes their families) made snacks and other nutritious edibles for organizations in need, such as the Ronald McDonald House and Family Focus, which also received baskets of goods from the Club for distribution during the holidays. Today, the Club staffs the First Presbyterian Church Soup Kitchen six Saturdays a year, preparing, reheating, and serving food.

In addition to providing literal nourishment, the Club has also worked to nourish the soul through projects to improve morale and well-being in times of distress. For example, Valentine's Day tote bags containing books, teas, jewelry, chocolates, cosmetics, lotions, and other toiletries were created for women at Housing Opportunities for Women (HOW) and the YWCA's shelter for victims of domestic violence. In 1999, the women assembled Mother's Day baskets full of gifts, and the project evolved into a holiday party and a Mother's Day party for the women and children at HOW. The members focused on helping families by participating in an Adopt-a-Family program that provided cash and gifts to a single family in need. The Club participated in the YWCA Evanston/North Shore Community Café, a summit of several local organizations working to improve the status of women and girls in the area.

Safe Places

The Woman's Club of Evanston is committed to creating safe spaces for women in transition who need a bit of extra help in overcoming hardships and making it to the next stage of their lives. As the issue of domestic violence became more acknowledged in the wider society, the Club responded by providing funding to projects at places such as the Evanston YWCA Shelter for Battered Women and Their Children (Mary Lou's Place), HOW, and Deborah's Place. The Club worked closely with the YWCA and HOW to decorate rooms in the shelters (through the Adopt-A-Room initiative in 1999 and 2000), donate linens to the women living at these sites, provide resume writing workshops, and spearhead drives for clothing (particularly maternity clothing), food, formula, and diapers in addition to raising thousands of dollars for these groups through the annual benefit and other events. The October 2012 *Bulletin* included this description of the Adopt-A-Room program: "Members get together on a Saturday morning with good old-fashioned elbow grease to scrub, clean, organize, arrange, refresh, and redecorate a room, complete with new bedding, bath accessories, and gift bags for the resident mom and her children. The aim of this project is to help give these families a fresh new outlook."

Adopt-A-Room

In addition to supporting safe spaces, the Club donated to the Million Mom March, a rally against gun violence in Washington, DC, on May 14, 2000, and participated in the satellite event in downtown Chicago. The Club also participates in the Keep Evanston Beautiful TrashBusters program, an annual event to clear the streets of garbage and debris, which helps create a safe, serene space for all of Evanston's citizens.

Working mothers have long been a concern of the Club's, and the tradition has been carried on by supporting Family Focus, the Evanston Childcare Network, the Evanston Day Nursery Association, and numerous programs at the YMCA. In addition to raising funds for these organizations, the clubwomen have participated with hands-on volunteer hours. In 1994, the Club provided food for baskets at Thanksgiving and Christmas for the Family Focus Evanston Holiday Project and a toy drive has been conducted each year for this organization.

Long-standing relationships with the Infant Welfare Society of Evanston and Children's Home and Aid, established in Illinois in 1883, are documented throughout the Woman's Club archives. In a 1994 letter to then President Helen Lee Davis, David Kirk, president of the society, thanked the Club for a gift of $2,019.20: "At a time when our national agenda seems to focus so much on the media-hype surrounding healthcare, political ethics, and 'the system,' and so little on the daily challenges facing children and families on the local level, it's more crucial than ever that caring community members band together to take action." Another opportunity to fulfill this mission, in which the Auxiliary participated in the 1990s, was the Hug a Baby project at Cook County Hospital, and the Auxiliary continued to support the Northwestern University Settlement Association one hundred years after the Club first provided funds for its kindergarten.

The Club also supports the community's oldest citizens. In addition to the traditional parties and teas for seniors held throughout the years, the Club contributed volunteer hours to Presbyterian Homes, a local retirement community, during this period. Members socialized with residents, provided transportation to activities, and arranged and attended social hours. The members also conducted interviews with seniors at North Shore Village, a program created to provide services that enable seniors to remain independent in their own homes. These interviews were published on the Village's website.

Where Everyone Is Welcome

Recreational spaces and programs that allow children to play in positive, safe environments have received support from the Club since the early

1900s when the women helped to develop playgrounds in the Evanston and greater Chicago area.

The Club has been a strong supporter of the local YMCA even when Evanston had two separate facilities: a branch facility for "colored" citizens on Emerson Street and the main building on Grove for whites only. Club members contributed to both, including paying for memberships, developing after-school programs, and donating money over the years to ensure that all children in the community would have a safe space to learn and play.

This commitment continues today. In 2008 the Club contributed over $100,000 to specific programs run by the McGaw YMCA and the YWCA Evanston/North Shore. These programs include Camp Echo, the Diversity Initiative, and the Flying Fish Aquatics Scholarship Program (providing thirty full scholarships for two years). In 2017, the Woman's Club committed to supporting both organizations in a significant way with our largest directed fundraising events: the beneficiary of the 2018 Revue was the McGaw YMCA Men's Residence Program, and the 2018 spring benefit beneficiary was the YWCA's Bridges Longer Term Housing for Survivors of Domestic Abuse. Funds have also been given to the Night Ministry, a shelter and resource center for LGBT youth located on the north side of Chicago.

Fairy Tail Trail

The Club's most well-known project was the Fairy Tale Trail. Once upon a time, "a fairy tale began to unfold in Evanston when members of the Auxiliary met to discuss plans for a new community service project involving children with disabilities." The Club members did not know at the start that the work would ultimately benefit thousands of children of all abilities, both locally and nationally.

In the summer of 1988, Lekotek, a national nonprofit organization serving children with special needs through play-centered programs and toy libraries, asked the Auxiliary to create a Halloween House that would be accessible for local children with and without disabilities. At first, the members "envisioned the same small-scale church basement type events—minus the barriers. But as their creative juices started flowing, and with the help of the engineer elves of Lekotek who developed special gadgetry, concepts began to take shape. . . . It was an event that would not, could not, die." After two years of planning, involving 150 Auxiliary members and their families, along with sponsorships from local businesses and the Omni Orrington Hotel, which donated their ballroom, the plan came to fruition in October 1990.

Fairy Tale Trail logo

Jungle Room, Fairy Tale Trail, circa 1990–2000s

Three Bears Room, Fairy Tale Trail, circa 1990–2000s

The Fairy Tale Trail featured eight themed rooms based on children's stories, with costumed characters (volunteers and staff from the Auxiliary and Lekotek), and creative, sensory-stimulating activities. A flyer for the event read, "Look for hands-on, creative surprises in each room— and tricks and treats, too!" Both the Auxiliary and Lekotek envisioned this as an inclusive Halloween event. Sara Brenner, one of the organizers, explained, "At the Fairy Tale Trail, children with and without disabilities can share in the fun together, side by side." A couple of years into the project, a letter from Beth Boosalis Davis of Lekotek noted: "Not only was the event a record-breaking fundraiser, but it also provided a unique brand of Halloween joy to 3,000 Chicago-area children. It was especially heartening to see many families with children with special needs have the opportunity to participate—as a family—in this wonderful children's holiday." The Auxiliary and Lekotek felt that they had accomplished and even exceeded their expectations. Through their efforts at fantasy, not fright, they had designed the trail "from the perspective of *every* child" in order to "educat[e] and sensitiz[e] . . . children to the needs of their peers with special needs." An article in the *Chicago Tribune* reported, "At this house there are no creaky stairs to climb, out-of-reach doorbells to ring, or any other unintended 'tricks' that can make Halloween no treat at all for children with disabilities."

In the project's first year, 1,500 children attended, and a sum of $2,500 was raised for Lekotek. Word spread quickly. In its second year, the event drew 3,000 children, and the women raised $9,000. That year, Ronald McDonald Children's Charities donated $5,000 to the operation of the Trail. The women hosted numerous student groups and families, and by 1995, about 3,300 children were following the Trail each year. The Trail garnered so much attention that it received write-ups in the October 1991 issues of *Family Circle* and *Parenting* magazines and was featured on *Good Morning America* and local television stations. In 1991, Auxiliary members Julie Morse and Kathy Francis, organizers of the event in these first years, wrote a manual, *Creating a Barrier-Free Halloween House*, which was written up in several prominent magazines and received generous local news coverage, leading to the creation of at least five other barrier-free Halloween Houses in cities nationwide. By 1993, the Auxiliary was generating cash and in-kind donations from forty-five companies and stores and had attracted two hundred North Shore volunteers to staff the event.

None of this would have been possible without the Auxiliary's determination, planning, and teamwork, and it would also have profound and positive influences on the lives of those who worked on the project. In an article in *Chicago Parent*, Diana Nielander of Lekotek attributed the Fairy Tale Trail's success to "the collaboration, synergy and teamwork of the Auxiliary and volunteers who have 'a deep personal love for what they're doing.'" Complimentary letters from Lekotek and the final report submitted by the event's cochairs applauded the women. The report stated: "The event was an inspiring success for those of us who worked on this project, and a proud tribute to the Auxiliary as a whole, measured in terms of community service, fundraising and social interaction—the three areas integral to our organization's formal mission." The Fairy Tale Trail helped to demonstrate the Auxiliary's value to the community at least to one person, as Julie Morse and Kathy Hardy noted in their final report:

> Also significant was that the often stony-faced members
> of the media were unusually supportive and vocal in their
> praise of the event, as were local business leaders. . . .
> And one well-known community leader who grew up in
> Evanston and has known about the Auxiliary for years
> through members who are his friends and co-workers,
> actually apologized to Julie Morse—because up until then
> he said he had assumed that all we did was the show and
> some social events. He had no idea the Auxiliary was so
> committed to community service. He had no idea we were
> such a vital, community-spirited organization.

When the Omni Orrington was unable to commit to a date in 1997, the Auxiliary moved the Fairy Tale Trail to the ballroom in the clubhouse, which had by that time been modified to provide full accessibility. The Trail was funded with proceeds from a Preview Party, a California Pizza Kitchen fundraiser (through the Scrip program), an admission fee, and grants. On average, over 1,000 people attended the preview party and regular Trail hours combined. School groups continued to take field trips to the trail, which was also open during regular hours, providing family fun for all ages.

Education Is the Key

The Club's members recognize that education does not stop with the classroom; rather, student success depends on access to education and resources outside of the classroom that help them to be successful community members. Building on its belief that every child, regardless of background, deserves the chance to be fully successful in life, the Club has supported LINKS, a center providing clinical services, sex education, and counseling for kids along with the First Baptist Church of Evanston, Howard Area Community Center, and Blessed Agnes Church, in an effort to reduce the dropout rate of Latino high school students. Both the Club and Auxiliary have given financial support to the Foster Reading Center at the McGaw YMCA, which provides literacy training, tutoring, and guided reading to children. In 1996, the Auxiliary raised $24,000 for the I Have a Dream Foundation, a national program that promises college scholarships to underprivileged sixth graders who complete their studies and attend post-secondary schools. In 1999, the Soar Through the Century benefit dinner dance raised $43,500 for the YMCA's Project SOAR, a mentoring program for at-risk Evanston youth. The 2007 spring benefit dinner recipient was Youth Organization Umbrella, Inc. (YOU), which according to its website, "offer[s] a holistic set of services—from afterschool entertainment and mentoring to clinical counseling and crisis intervention—to ensure that out-of-school time is safe, healthy, and fun."

The Club has long supported efforts to provide practical employment skills to youth and others in need. The Youth Job Center of Evanston responded to a grant from the proceeds of the 1999 Benefit Show, by saying, "It was quite a happy moment in the life of our small but growing agency. . . $25,000 is one of the largest grants we have ever received and it will go a long way toward helping us improve our programs. In particular we hope to use it to help us set up our in-house Graduate Equivalency Diploma (GED) and Basic Computer Skills program so badly needed here."

The Club also provides scholarships directly to those in need. Beginning in 1990, the Club set aside funds each year for two or three women applicants receiving GEDs who showed exceptional promise in continuing their studies. In a 1991 thank-you letter to then President Ginny Blair, one of the recipients said, "I am thrilled to be one of the awarded recipients for the $750.00 scholarship. I take great pride in my work and I appreciate any help from the community. Any form of encouragement is accepted, because returning to school is not an easy task. Both my academic and career goals in business are very important in my life." Another wrote, in 1994: "Thank you for not brushing me off as 'post graduate.' Thank you for a chance to accomplish my dreams. Thank you for recognizing my accomplishments. Thank you for giving me the chance to make a future for my children and myself." The Auxiliary earmarked the proceeds of the sales of their *Once Upon a Thyme* cookbook for scholarships to Evanston Township High School graduating students. Students who demonstrated a commitment to community service received awards of several hundred dollars. This scholarship was later renamed the Linda Wade Community Service Award, in honor of an Auxiliary member who passed away from leukemia at a young age.

Continuing the Legacy

The Charitable Foundation Trustees reevaluated their focus and impact between 2005 and 2010, developing a new mission statement:

> The Charitable Foundation of the Woman's Club of
> Evanston will invest in early childhood education.
> Research overwhelmingly shows that birth to five are
> vitally important and impactful years in a child's life. We
> will support programs that provide a continuity of care
> and education, thereby addressing the unfortunate gap in
> funding that exists for many families.

With this redefined focus, there was a renewed spirit of commitment and purpose. The Charitable Foundation continues to support the WCE Sewing Circle and the Linda Wade Community Service Award but has added annual scholarships to the Learning Bridge Early Education Center and Cherry Preschool.

In 2010, the trustees announced the creation of the Harbert Society, a special community of supporters of the Woman's Club of Evanston. It is named after and in honor of the exceptional work of Elizabeth Harbert when she gathered friends and neighbors at her house in 1889 for the

Charitable Foundation/Lily of the Valley pins given to members

purpose of bettering their communities. The Harbert Society was established to recognize individuals who have included the WCE in their estate plans. The Charitable Foundation created the Harbert Society and has taken on the responsibility of administrating it, launching an initiative to encourage and document planned gifts. To date there are more than forty-five Harbert Society members, who each received a lily of the valley pin styled after the flower worn by Harbert in her formal oil portrait.

The Club now establishes a particular "funding focus" each year in order to direct fundraising efforts into one general area, honoring organizations that reflected its founding principle of strengthening the Evanston community by addressing its most pressing needs. The annual Benefit Show, now called the WCE Revue, continues to raise tens of thousands of dollars for designated beneficiaries, which have included the James B. Moran Center for Youth Advocacy (2014), the Lilac Tree (2015), Family Matters (2016), Literature for All of Us (2017), the YMCA Men's Residence Program (2018), and Girls Play Sports (2019). The annual Spring Benefit dinner raises a similar sum annually, the most recent beneficiaries being Evanston Scholars (2014), the Harbor (2015), Curt's Café South (2016), Peer Health Exchange (2017), YWCA Bridges for Longer Term Housing for Domestic Violence Survivors (2018), and, in 2019, the beneficiary will be our own clubhouse.

HOW
Holiday Party

*Dreams Delivered
collection*

Evanston Day of Caring

These events depend on all the Club members contributing their time, talents, and efforts. The annual Benefit Show also includes the recipients of the proceeds in the planning and performance of the event. For the 2011 Benefit Show, the online news site *Evanston Now* reported Lucia Guridi, WCE Benefit Show producer, saying: "We are thrilled to have five staff members and three dedicated volunteers from Children's Home and Aid in the cast for our Diamond Anniversary Benefit Show. They are contributing their time and talent to sing, dance, and write for the show. Additionally, children from the Rice Child and Family Center's Expressive Therapy program are making some of our show props." The members work to actively involve the organizations they are supporting, rather than just handing over checks.

This personal connection is further demonstrated by ongoing volunteer activities including Deacon's Closet, Dreams Delivered Prom Boutique, Family Focus Toy Drive, YWCA Battered Women's Shelter Adopt-A-Room, the Sewing Circle (formerly Welfare Sewing), First Presbyterian Soup Kitchen, Housing Opportunities for Women (HOW) Holiday Party, YWCA/North Shore's Race against Hate, and Evanston School Children Clothing Assistance (ESCCA). The Club contributes over 15,000 volunteer hours annually on projects meant to increase community well-being and foster personal connections and relationships. In the Dreams Delivered Prom Boutique, the young recipients receive an in-person experience with individuals who truly care about their well-being—in addition to a beautiful dress. The Sewing Circle continues hand-creating unique, high-quality articles, and it ranks second only to toy drives as the longest-standing organized volunteer activity in the Club's history. They plan and participate in parties for HOW as well as hosting a holiday party for Deacon's Closet.

For decades, the Club has raised funds in collaboration with local businesses, targeting portions of sales for worthy causes. Today's version is the Scrip Program, whereby members purchase gift cards to a variety of businesses, with the Club receiving a percentage of the sales of these gift cards.

The proceeds from both the Holiday Bazaar Gift Fair (formerly Cornucopia Gift Fair) and the annual yearbook go into the General Fund, which funds the annual grants awarded by the Contributions Committee each year. In addition, the Club has a FUNdraising committee that creates fun and social events, such as BINGO nights or Zumba classes, to raise money for the General Fund.

In 2017–2018, the Club awarded grants to the following organizations:

- Beyond the Baby Blues

- Boys Hope Girls Hope of Illinois

- Center for Independent Futures

- Evanston Township High School Health Center

- The Floured Apron

- Holy Spirit Life Learning Center

- Howard Area Community Center

- Institute for Psychoanalysis/Barr-Harris Children's Grief Center

- Interfaith Action of Evanston

- The Lilac Tree

- Northlight Theatre

- Open Studio Project

- She Is Code

- Turning Point Behavioral Health Care Center

- Youth Organization Umbrella, Inc. (Y.O.U.)

The Club's success clearly depends on the hard work and determination of its members. Any woman is welcome to join, with membership requirements balancing philanthropy, service, and friendship. Each member must pay annual dues, serve on a chosen committee that meets once a month and drives the Club's programming and decision making, participate in two community outreach projects each year, support the major philanthropic projects (through planning, staffing, purchasing, and/or selling admission tickets), and attend social functions, because, as it's put on the Club's website, "it is the good times we share and the friendships we make that make our Club so special." Workshops and meetings for new and prospective members are held several times throughout the year and women are encouraged to attend events or participate in projects to make sure that the Club is right for them. Women of all ages and backgrounds make up the membership, and all are welcomed with open arms. Group volunteer activities help to form these bonds; the laughter of script readings or dressing up as a fairy tale character is an unparalleled experience. As Leslie Sevcik, 2004 Cornucopia Chair said in the *Bulletin*, "Throughout the five-day decorating, setup, and three-day show, I repeatedly witnessed new and established members forming new friendships as they worked together at Cornucopia. . . . I was also gratified to see women of all ages and backgrounds working together so well, and having such fun doing it." The recently formed Members Assistance Team works to ensure that members falling on hard times have a strong support network to keep them going.

While the Club depends on the work, talents, skills and contributions of its individual members, none of its accomplishments could be possible without the collective spirit, the collaboration, the friendships, the networks, and the bonds among members. Smaller fundraisers emphasize fun and philanthropy. Programming on topics ranging from food to travel to book reviews to current events blends the social and the educational. Also in the mix, of course, are the purely social occasions that allow women to meet and form the bonds that lead to amazing work in the community. It is in these spaces that new, innovative ideas are created through collaboration with others. Recipe tastings, bridge games, fashion shows, summer parties, field trips, and countless teas, desserts, luncheons, and dinners—the friendships and bonds—are the glue that keeps the Club together.

At times, the Club has been forced to eschew its "tea drinking" image to prove its value in the face of doubters; but it is the tea drinking, the wine drinking, the dances, and the dinners that truly hold the Club together and enable it to most effectively carry out its commitment to improve the community. By forming both personal and professional networks with other women, members develop the leadership skills to be forces for positive change. Today, women can vote, take on leadership positions in the workforce, and choose whether to marry or have children. But women-only spaces continue to provide essential systems of support that help women maintain the status they have always deserved but which took so long to achieve.

The Club partnered with the YWCA/North Shore and Northwestern University's Women's Center to initiate the first International Women's Day celebration in Evanston in 2010, and March 2017 marked the seventh IWD celebration, showing increased growth and participation every year since its inception.

Looking to the Future

The women who founded this Club were committed to social justice, equality, and the rights of women. They felt it was their civic duty and obligation to contribute to their community. We must continue their mission to provide more opportunities to make Evanston and surrounding communities better places for all women—for our mothers, daughters, grandmothers, sisters, aunts, and nieces. We owe it to them, we owe it to ourselves.

—Beth Geiger
President, 2012–2013

A 2012 article in *Crain's Chicago Business* reported women's clubs in the area were struggling to stay relevant and alive, to prove their necessity in the community. Not so for the Woman's Club of Evanston. According to the article,

> many of the Clubs look wistfully at the Woman's Club of Evanston, which boasts 400 members and a Clubhouse that's sought after by brides and Northwestern University event planners. Much the way the Union League of Chicago has survived with diverse programming, so has the Evanston Club. Numerous fundraisers help fuel its philanthropic efforts—the organization doles out $125,000 annually to community groups. There also is a mix of programming: intellectual discussions, dramatizations or important historical events, and enrichment programs.

Unlike some Clubs, there's no sponsorship to join and no requirement to be super-involved. The Woman's Club also has a deep bench of professional women on its membership rolls.

That is not to say that the Club has not had its struggles. Some people believe the work of the Woman's Club is finished. Much of what we take for granted today in order to live healthy, happy lives was started by women's clubs all over the nation, and now that these systems are in place, what is the need for these organizations of women? Clubhouses are expensive to maintain, women are busy juggling all their life commitments, and the needs of others are taken care of by established agencies.

However, the Club's work is far from over. Whenever funding and support for social services and health agencies has dropped, the Woman's Club of Evanston has stepped in to raise hundreds of thousands of dollars to ensure that these groups can continue to help those in need, especially women and children. These organizations and agencies could not have started without the tireless efforts of women reformers seeking to better the lives of all individuals, regardless of background, and they cannot fully continue without the Club's help.

The Club's work is not just about writing checks or holding fundraisers. Money alone cannot impact the lives of beneficiaries. Recognizing that healing begins with the formation of relationships, connections, and friendships, the Club works to provide a support network and to let people know that there are those who care enough about them to sew infant layettes, decorate rooms in their temporary residences, and bake healthy snacks from their own kitchens. Social service agencies depend on individuals and organizations coming forward to fill in the gaps that the money leaves behind—the personal touch and connection that is missing when a check is handed over. Throughout its history, Club members have not simply spent money on a milk inspector, but visited dairies; have not simply given money to hospitals in the aftermath of wars, but threw holiday parties and delivered handmade goods to soldiers; have not only bought new clothing for schoolchildren, but also spent countless hours sewing outfits, collecting suitcases full of necessities, and helping to outfit girls in the foster system; have not only purchased or made food for those who are hungry, but also delivered and served it.

Why has the Woman's Club of Evanston survived while similar groups have been forced to disband? The two key factors that have kept the Club going are the clubhouse and the friendships. The former provides an inviting place for the members to come together to form those vital friendships. Friendship is sometimes considered merely a by-product of membership in the Club, second to its work in the community, but without the teas, brunches, dinners, and programs that promote solidarity among these women, their work would never be successfully carried out. The Club, in turn, draws on these friendships and networks to expand its membership and support its ongoing commitments to the Evanston community. Each woman brings her own unique perspective and talent, ensuring that the Club's work is as successful as it can be in helping to make a difference.

What was once a club that focused exclusively on who you knew has grown into an organization that provides a supportive space to nurture, encourage, and develop each member's own interests, talents, and leadership skills so that each member can, through collaboration with others, make a positive impact on the community. If the Club is only as strong as its weakest link, then the current active membership of more than 350, far outnumbering any women's club in the immediate area, combined with over $125,000 in annual charitable donations and a calendar full of educational and entertaining programming, can attest to the strength of its members. From its earliest days, the Club has been made up of women who are determined to use their talents and skills to make a positive difference in their community, women who are not content to sit by and let others do the work for them. Women of all different backgrounds and professions who know that they can be a force for good in their community support the Club's many activities, from clubhouse maintenance, to fundraising, to program planning, to community outreach and volunteering, and more. These women—and their successors—will take the Club into its future and beyond, faithfully carrying out its motto:

In essentials, unity; in non-essentials, liberty; in all things, charity.

Epilogue
The 125th Anniversary Year: 2013–2014

A 125th Anniversary Celebration Committee was commissioned by Club President Mimi Roeder in 2008 to plan and execute a Club year of celebration. The committee's mission:

> *To Commemorate our 125th Anniversary, Celebrate our history, Communicate who we are and Contribute to our Community!*

The 125th anniversary of the Woman's Club was celebrated throughout the 2013–2014 Club year with member activities, community events, and a dedicated goal to give $125,000 back to our community.

THE WOMAN'S CLUB OF EVANSTON

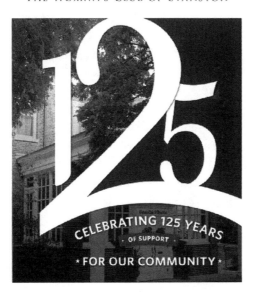

To commemorate our anniversary, a timeline history of the Club was compiled, covering the founding of the Club (1889) through the building of the clubhouse (1912–1913), the formation of the Young Woman's Auxiliary (1943), the creation of the Charitable Foundation (1968), the Capital Campaign (2005), and our inclusion on the National Register of Historic Places (2006). This book, *The Woman's Club of Evanston: A History*, was proposed and ultimately commissioned for development in 2011.

In December 2013, the Club received two proclamations in honor of the 125th anniversary: one from the State of Illinois and one from the City of Evanston. The State of Illinois proclamation recognized the Club as a leading nonprofit organization on the North Shore that responds to the local needs of the community by advancing philanthropic, educational, cultural, and humanitarian principles and activities. At the annual holiday dinner, Thomas Choi, Public Affairs Manager for Illinois State Comptroller Judy Baar Topinka, read the proclamation. Evanston Mayor Elizabeth Tisdahl surprised Club members while reading the city's proclamation when she stated: "Now therefore, I, Elizabeth B. Tisdahl, Mayor of the City of Evanston, do hereby proclaim December 11, 2013, as 'Woman's Club of Evanston Day' in the City of Evanston in celebration of their 125th anniversary."

Kathy Rocklin (President, 2013–2014) hosted a community reception in February 2014 that was attended by representatives of many past and current beneficiaries, Evanston dignitaries, and past Club presidents. Producers of the cable network show *The Reporters* were present and conducted interviews with beneficiaries and documented the reception. This footage was incorporated into a documentary, *The Woman's Club of Evanston—Making a Difference*, and broadcast on Evanston's cable channel in 2015. It featured the 125-year history of the Club and communicated who we are as a Club.

In addition, Rocklin created a time capsule in honor of the 125th anniversary, which included a copy of the documentary, the Club's membership roster, the annual yearbook highlighting both the anniversary year and the Benefit Show, and a message book signed by current Club members, community leaders, and beneficiaries with messages to those who will open the time capsule. The time capsule is housed in the Club archives.

Contents of the Time Capsule Created March 2014

Green Book
  This includes a current membership roster, bylaws, board of directors, officers from date of organization, and more.

Yearbook
  The program from the Annual Benefit Show highlights both the show and the 125th anniversary year. It was set up as flip book to showcase the anniversary on one side and the Benefit Show on the other.

The Woman's Club of Evanston—Making a Difference
  A DVD produced by the cable network show *The Reporters* in 2015.

Signature book containing messages from current Club members and community leaders and beneficiaries.

Commemorative booklet for the 125th anniversary in 2014.

Commemorative booklet for the 100th anniversary in 1989.

Invitation to the Past President's Policy Dinner, September 11, 2013.

List of donors to the 125th Anniversary Celebration Fund, as of September 15, 2013.

Invitation to the Community Reception, February 19, 2014.

Evanston RoundTable newspaper dated February 27, 2014, with article about the Community Reception that took place on February 19.

Card announcing International Women's Day 2014, an event held at the Club March 7, 2014.

Invitation to a reception at Elizabeth Boynton Harbert's house, April 27, 2014.

Invitation to the Woman's Club Spring Benefit, May 3, 2014.

Invitation to the 2014 Program for Annual Dinner, May 15, 2014.

DVD of photographs from 2013–2014; the photographs were shown during the Annual Dinner, May 15, 2014.

Brochure for the Contributions to Our Community Breakfast, May 28, 2014.

Packet of seeds such as was provided to each attendee of the Contributions breakfast.

Toothpick displays honoring the 125th anniversary.

A copy of the *Chicago Tribune*, December 29, 2013, with the article "Top U.S. Stories of 2013."

Two copies of the *Evanston Magazine* from two editions of the *Evanston RoundTable*, with the articles "15 Stories—150 Years" and "The City We Love—1863–2013," which mentions the WCE.

Coins dated 2014—a penny, a nickel, a dime, and a quarter.

Assembled by Kathy Rocklin, President of the Woman's Club of Evanston, 2013–14

Internally, the Club continued to make a difference. In 2014, the name of the Welfare Sewing Committee was changed to the Sewing Circle, and the group began a new project in 2016: Dress a Girl Around the World. This project, a campaign undertaken in 2006 by Hope4Women International to bring dignity to women around the world, was brought to the Sewing Circle by Club member Adrienne Woodside. The Sewing Circle decided to support this mission and began making dresses. The Club also implemented a program to increase recycling efforts within the Club for both member events and private Club rentals.

In another event to celebrate the history, the past presidents were invited to tour Elizabeth Boynton Harbert's house, which still stands on Judson Street in Evanston, on a Sunday afternoon in April. Amanda Jones Hartnett, whose mother, Eloise, was a longtime Club member, graciously opened the house for an afternoon of conversation about Harbert and the founding of the Woman's Club.

To fulfill the goal of communicating about the Club both internally and externally, an increased use of social media—a Twitter feed, a public Facebook page, and a new Woman's Club Events Facebook page—was implemented by the Marketing Committee, as well as efforts to increase coverage in the local papers. The Club provided members with lawn signs commemorating the anniversary, which could be seen around town. Two Club programs, The History of the Clubhouse and Notable Women in the Woman's Club History, were held, and the annual High Tea for all members was revived in March 2014.

Finally, to contribute to the community, the Club continued supporting many community activities, including the Soup Kitchen, Fairy Tale Trail, Dreams Delivered, and the Family Focus Toy Drive. The legacy of 125 years of giving was honored with the 2013–2014 Giving Focus for grants to organizations reflecting our founding principle of strengthening our community by contributing over $125,000 to local nonprofits that year.

Strategic Planning for the Future

In 2004, a strategic plan, developed by outside consultants and brought to the Board of Directors, was put together in support of the Capital

We are on Instagram!

@TheWCofE

Campaign. The Club began to think more strategically. The five-year plan, begun in 2009 and culminating at the end of the 125th anniversary, included goals for each committee as well as specific tasks directed to achieving the goals. It revolved around five areas of focus:

- Organize for success

- Retain the members

- Showcase the Club

- Manage the finances responsibly

- Build the support infrastructure

So what was next? In 2013, the Bylaws/Strategic Planning Committee reviewed and evaluated the 2009 strategic plan to determine which goals had been met and, of the items that remained had not been completed, which were still desirable to pursue. Overall, the plan had been very successful, and many of the goals set for the 2009–2014 time frame had been reached. It was time to begin developing the next plan to address current needs and take the Club into the future.

The Bylaws/Strategic Planning Committee began looking at a major restructuring of the committees around the core Club activities: fundraising, volunteering, member events, and administration. Committees would be grouped into functional areas allowing for cross-project collaboration and unified goals.

This new strategic plan was developed as a three-year plan, and it included the adoption of a new Club mission statement: *Connecting women behind a shared purpose of volunteerism, social empowerment, and community support.* It also called for approval of funding for a new branding initiative. In March 2015, the membership unanimously approved the new strategic plan, including the addition of leadership positions and some revisions to the bylaws.

In November 2014, the Board of Directors approved the key components of the new strategic plan, including the addition of leadership positions which were added to the 2015–2016 nominating process. The end result was that the Board of Directors was streamlined to enable more efficient strategic management and the organization became more flexible and adaptable. The Board of Directors was reduced in size to include the following positions:

Executive Leadership
President
President Elect
Treasurer
Secretary (nonvoting member)

Core Club Functions
Membership Chair
Philanthropy Chair
Community Outreach Chair

Administration and Operations
House and Grounds Chair
Marketing and Communications Chair
Bylaws and Strategic Planning Chair

The standing committees and various other committees were aligned to connect the chairs of the Club's major initiatives—Membership, Community Outreach, and Philanthropy—into functional areas. This new group is called the Leadership Council. The Leadership Council ideally comes together to discuss future planning, strategic ideas, calendar coordination, collaboration, and other important issues related to their activities and the Club as a whole.

These meetings are facilitated by the executive committee chair for each area:

Membership
> Assistant Membership (Recruiting)
> Programs
> Social and Enrichment
> Member Assistance Team (MAT)

Philanthropy
> Assistant Philanthropy Chair
> WCE Revue (formerly the Benefit Show)
> Yearbook
> Spring Benefit
> WCE Holiday Bazaar (formerly Cornucopia)
> FUN'draising

Community Outreach
> Assistant Community Outreach Chair
> External Volunteer Coordinator
> Contributions
> Fairy Tale Trail
> Dreams Delivered

The board also approved the addition of the leadership positions to the Office of the President, which appoints members into these roles:

Sponsorship/Donor Coordinator—coordinates sponsorship/ donor development and Clubwide tracking to help streamline the process

Technology Manager—organizes and implements communications to be used on the website

Finance Advisory Council Committee (FSAC) Chair—
represents an advisory committee to the Board of Directors
on matters pertaining to investments and long-term financial planning

Archives Chair—oversees the archives and adds new information annually

Committee charters were written and approved by the board during the
2015–2016 Club year and covered each committee's statement of purpose, organizational structure, and its duties and responsibilities.

Branding: Reimaging

To ensure that the Club remained relevant and compelling to current
and prospective members, it was also time to refresh the Club's brand
identity. The Bylaws/Strategic Planning Committee recommended qualities for which the Club should be known: friendship, empowerment, and
community support. In addition, four core messages were articulated that
are perceived as making the Woman's Club of Evanston unique:

Varied women with a shared purpose
Build lifelong friendships
Grow leaders
Have fun while doing good

As part of the effort, the Club developed a brand logo and tagline for
the public face of the Woman's Club, representing the Club to prospective members as well as potential business partners and sponsors. The logo
embraces one of the club colors—green—but in a fresh way. The prominent W subtly calls to mind a volunteer ribbon, representing the core mission of service. But the design as a whole also illustrates that the membership is a group of women making a difference in the lives of others while
forming lasting relationships and helping to build leaders along the way.
The original WCE crest, developed in 1917, was not retired; it was determined that it remains valuable to Club members and should continue to
be used internally for appropriate formal and historical occasions, as it still
represents the founding principles of unity, charity, and liberty.

New logo, 2015

Always Open to Reorganizing the Organization

The Bylaws/Strategic Planning Committee presented further changes to the leadership structure by proposing that the House and Grounds Chair make a one-year commitment, with the addition of an ascending Assistant House and Grounds Chair, the same structure that was already in place for the other functional areas.

Ad hoc committees were created early in fiscal year 2016 to review major Club events and take a look at long-term clubhouse needs for effectiveness, return on investment, and member engagement, as well as annual timing and alignment with strategic statements of friendship, leadership, and community. One result of these committee meetings was the decision to discontinue Fairy Tale Trail after twenty-five years. The last Fairy Tale Trail was held in October 2015, the event was put on hiatus in 2016, and it was officially ended in 2017. The Board of Directors decided it was in the best interest of the Club to look forward and to explore new projects that will allow the Club to grow and thrive as an organization.

The newly implemented changes are constantly evaluated and assessed. Further updates and changes may be proposed, discussed, and implemented in the future. Ultimately, the goal is to empower the Club's leadership and membership to make impactful strategic decisions to ensure that we are managing our resources to serve the community and the membership in the best way possible.

Dream House Project: This Old House, Part III

In 2015, under the direction of President Jan Hartwell, President Elect Chava Wu, the board, and the House and Grounds Chair, an ad hoc committee was established to take a long-term, strategic look at the maintenance needs of the clubhouse. The committee was named the Dream House Committee, and its goal was to create a unified aesthetic for the building by creating a master plan for the clubhouse, incorporating all anticipated maintenance and repairs as well as needed updates.

An interior design firm, M. Lavender Interior Design and Project Management, was selected in September 2016 to work with the Dream House Committee to develop the plan. The master plan prioritizes maintenance, repairs, and renovation projects and includes architectural drawings, timelines, finishes, cost estimates, and schedules. It was completed in the winter of 2017 and approved by the board in the late spring of 2017. The plan calls for a phased construction approach to minimize the impact on members and on Club events and operations. The full project will take three to five years, and when it is complete, the WCE clubhouse will boast a completely renovated interior with new member meeting areas, restrooms, carpet, paint, light fixtures, and furnishings.

Phase 1 of the master plan began with construction in November 2017 and was completed by March 2018. The first phase included renovations to the first- and second-floor bathrooms, expanding the facilities with gender-neutral private bathrooms and updating the fixtures. Additionally, the floor in the sunroom was raised to the same height as the adjacent tea room, and new flooring, furniture, and window treatments were added. Retractable pocket doors were installed to allow a section of the sunporch to be closed off, creating a flexible space for member use or meetings.

Future phases of the master plan will bring more fresh paint and a unified color scheme as the Club purchases new furnishings and carpet, refurbishes the marble floors and the stairwell, and installs new lighting throughout the Club.

Last Words

This book captures the continuing story of the Woman's Club of Evanston. We are deeply grateful to all who came before us, who built and sustained the Club through decades of immense change, and we are thankful to be a part of the legacy now, indebted to those who will follow, upholding the mission to connect women behind a shared purpose of volunteerism, social empowerment, and community support as we move through the next century.

Former Presidents shall be Honorary Members of the Club.

Mrs. Elizabeth Boynton Harbert* 1889–1897

Mrs. T. P. Stanwood* 1897–1899

Mrs. Richard H. Wyman* 1899–1901

Mrs. H. H. Kingsley* 1901–1902

Mrs. C. A. Goodnow* 1902–1904

Mrs. Towner K. Webster* 1904–1906

Mrs. B. A. Green* 1906–1907

Mrs. Charles S. Raddin* 1907–1909

Mrs. Ulysses S. Grant* 1909–1911

Mrs. Charles E. Clifton* 1911–1913

Mrs. Rufus C. Dawes* 1913–1915

Mrs. Leslie E. Hildreth* 1915–1917

Mrs. John Harper Long* 1917–1919

Mrs. G. W. Kaufmann* 1919–1921

Mrs. Robert Berry Ennis* 1921–1923

Mrs. William G. Alexander* 1923–1924

Mrs. Charles H. Betts* 1924–1926

Mrs. Wirt E. Humphrey* 1926–1927

Mrs. Charles W. Spofford* 1927–1929

Mrs. Robert L. Elliott* 1929–1931

Mrs. Bruce Scott* 1931–1933

Mrs. Walter Delano Burr* 1933–1935

Mrs. Edison B. Fowler* 1935–1937

Mrs. William C. Gilbert* 1937–1939

Mrs. Charles C. Wells* 1939–1941

Mrs. Edward R. Ladd* 1941–1943

Mrs. Orno B. Roberts* 1943–1945

Mrs. Arthur E. Swanson* 1945–1947

Mrs. I. A. Smothers* 1947–1949

Mrs. Douglas Kirkpatrick* 1949–1950

Mrs. Eugene M. Stearns* 1951–1953

Mrs. Horace Dawson* 1953–1955

Mrs. Wesley W. Race* 1955–1957

Mrs. William N. Erickson* 1957–1959

Mrs. Otho E. Scott* 1959–1961

Mrs. Norman E. H. Deletzke* 1961–1963

Mrs. Douglas D. Waitley* 1963–1965

Mrs. Fred I. Norman* 1965–1967

Mrs. Herbert E. Mueller* 1967–1969

Mrs. James Loring Peirce* 1969–1971

Mrs. Bailey Martin* 1971–1973

Mrs. Frank M. Mason, Jr.* 1973–1975

Mrs. Arthur G. Freeman 1975–1977

Mrs. William Onderdonk, Jr.* 1977–1979

Mrs. V. Robbins Tate, Jr. 1979–1981

Mrs. Ellerth Overboe* 1981–1983

Mrs. Redmond P. Hogan* 1983–1985

Mrs. Ray M. Wiese* 1985–1987

Mrs. Emil G. Graff* 1987–1989

Mrs. Warden T. Blair Jr.* 1989–1991

Mrs. Garth J. Conley* 1991–1993

Mrs. John R. Davis* 1993–1995

Mrs. George L. Landgren 1995–1997

Mrs. Henry L. Anderson* 1997–1999

Mrs. W. Daniel Wefler 1999–2000

Ms. Vickie Burke 2000–2001

Ms. Diane Golan 2001–2002

Ms. Nancy Cunniff 2002–2003

Ms. Trimble Stamell 2003–2004

Ms. Wendy Holstead Irwin 2004–2005

Ms. Jane Ann DeMoss 2005–2006

Ms. Patricia Shaw Sprague 2006–2007

Ms. Mimi Roeder 2007–2008

Ms. Terry Dason 2008–2009

Ms. Julie Singer Chernoff 2009–2010

Ms. Tamara McKnight 2010–2011

Ms. Anne Johnson Gilford 2011–2012

Ms. Beth Geiger 2012–2013

Ms. Kathy Rocklin 2013–2014

Ms. Anita Remijas 2014–2015

Ms. Jan Hartwell 2015–2016

Ms. Chava Wu 2016–2017

Ms. Rona Green Taylor 2017–2018

Ms. Melanie Cody 2018–2019

*deceased

TIMELINE

1851	Northwestern University is founded.
1863	Evanston incorporates as a town.
1868	Women's clubs are founded in New York City and Boston.
1889	Harbert invites women to gather in her home.
March 23, 1889	First official meeting of the Woman's Club of Evanston
1892	Evanston incorporates as a city. The Club donates money to help start Evanston Community Hospital.
1897	Elizabeth Boynton Harbert delivers her resignation speech at the clubhouse. The Club starts its welfare sewing and visiting nurse programs.
1902	The mobile library is established.
1910	The Club votes to give one-tenth of its income to charity.
March 25, 1911	The cornerstone is laid for the building of the clubhouse.
1913	The clubhouse opens.
1914	The first Art Show takes place.
1917–1918	The Community Kitchen opens.
1943	The Young Woman's Auxiliary is formed.
1951	The annual Benefit Show begins.
1952	The Club sponsors Evanston's first Mothers March on Polio as part of the March of Dimes campaign.
1965	The first Antique Show is held.
1968	The Charitable Foundation is created.
1987	The Merry Merry Market is established. It later evolves into Cornucopia and then the Holiday Bazaar.
1990	Fairy Tale Trail is created.
1991	The Club reinstates its policy of having a designated beneficiary for the annual Benefit Show and Spring Benefit Dinner Dance.
1999–2000	Dissolution of the Young Woman's Auxiliary and merger with the Woman's Club of Evanston.
2005	Capital Campaign and the first year of the Dreams Delivered program.
2006	Clubhouse is added to the National Register of Historic Places.
2011	*The Woman's Club of Evanston: A History* is proposed and ultimately comissioned.
2014	125th Anniversary of the establishment of the Club

1. "A New Woman's Club," *Evanston Index*, March 9, 1889; quoted in "Reminiscences of 30 Years," 1920, p. 8, Women's Club of Evanston, Northwestern University Library.

2. Diana B. Turk, *Bound by a Mighty Vow: Sisterhood and Women's Fraternities, 1870–1920* (New York: New York University Press, 2004), p. 14–15.

3. Harriet Clifton, "The Woman's Club and Its Relation to the Community," Evanston News, September 13, 1911.

4. Alli Jason, Louise Strickland, and Margaret McMillen, *Women in the Progressive Era: A Unit of Study for Grades 9–12* (Los Angeles: National Center for History in the Schools, UCLA, n.d.) p. 17. Originally published: Grover Cleveland, "Woman's Mission and Woman's Clubs," *Ladies Home Journal* 22 (May 1905), p. 3.

5. Maude G. Palmer, *History of the Illinois Federation of Women's Clubs 1894–1928* (Chicago: Illinois Federation of Women's Clubs, 1928), p. 13.

6. William Blair, *Making and Remaking Pennsylvania's Civil War* (University Park: Pennsylvania State University Press, 2000), p. 273.

7. Karen Blair, *The Clubwoman as Feminist: True Womanhood Redefined, 1868–1914* (New York: Holmes & Meier, 1980).

8. Ruth Bordin, *Woman and Temperance: The Quest for Power and Liberty, 1873–1900* (Philadelphia: Temple University Press, 1981).

9. Ibid.

10. Blair, *The Clubwoman as Feminist*, p. 15.

11. Julia Ward Howe, "How Can Women Best Associate?" in *Papers and Letters Presented at the First Woman's Congress of the Association for the Advancement of Woman* (New York: Mrs. Wm. Ballard, 1874).

12. Ibid., pp. 6–7.

13. Clifton, "The Woman's Club and Its Relation to the Community."

14. Later documents indicate that Roberts Rules of Order were used in Club meetings, but we have no early evidence of this.

15. *Evanston Press*, April 27, 1889.

16. David Waltz, "In Essentials, Unity; in Non-essentials, Liberty; in All Things, Charity," Articuli Fidei [blog], December 9, 2010, http://articulifidei .blogspot.com/2010/12/in-essentials-unity-in-non-essentials.html.

17. There is a letter in the black scrapbook in the clubhouse from Frances Willard, thanking the Club for this honor. In those days, the Club did not meet during the summer months; the Club year ended in May. Now the Club year starts in June and goes through May, although the summer months are still considered "quiet" by Club standards.

18. Cindy Koenig Richards, "The Awakening: Rhetoric and the Rise of New Women in the New Northwest, 1868–1912" (Doctoral diss., Northwestern University, 2008), ProQuest (3303641).

19. Jane Cunningham Croly, *The History of the Woman's Club Movement in America* (New York: Henry G. Allen, 1898)

20. See Mary Jean Houde, *Reaching Out: A Story of the General Federation of Women's Clubs* (Chicago: Mobium Press, 1989).

21. Chicago Commons Association, *The Commons: A Monthly Record Devoted to Aspects of Life and Labor* 2 (June 1897), p. 10.; "Meeting of Evanston Woman's Club: Mrs. Elizabeth Boynton Harbert Resigns as President and Is Succeed by Mrs. Stanwood," *Chicago Daily Tribune*, April 17, 1897, p. 3.

22. Chicago Commons Association Executive Committee, *Chicago Commons: A Social Settlement* (Chicago, March 1899). http://libsysdigi .library.illinois.edu/oca/Books2007-09/chicagocommonsso00chic/ chicagocommonsso00chic.pdf.

23. John W. Trask, "Milk and Its Relation to Infectious Diseases," *Journal of the American Medical Association* 51, no. 2 (October 31, 1908), 1493.

24. For more information, see John A. Glover and Royce R. Ronning, *Historical Foundations of Education Psychology* (New York: Plenum Press, 1987); George Pliny Brown, George Alfred Brown, and William Chandler Bagley, *School and Home Education*, vol. 20 (Bloomington, IL: Public-School Publishing Company, 1901), p. xvi; Palmer, *History of the Illinois Federation of Women's Clubs*; and Illinois Society for Child-Study, *The Child-Study Monthly*, vol. 3, ed. William O. Krohn and Alfred Bayliss (Chicago: A. W. Mumford, 1897), p. 211.

25. For more information, see The Club Woman, vol. 10, no. 1 (March 1903), p. 242; Mrs. William F. Hefferan, "Mrs. Roger B. McMullen [biographical essay]," *School and Home Education*, vol. 35 (December 1915, pp. 116–17; Ellen Lee Wyman, "Illinois Mothers' Congress," *Kindergarten Magazine*, vol. 13, no. 1 (September 1900), pp. 41–46.

26. Charlene K. Haar, *The Politics of the PTA* (New Brunswick, NJ: Transaction Publishers, 2002), 40.

27. Louise Brockway Stanwood, "Charitable Associations," in *History of Northwestern University and Evanston*, ed. Robert D. Sheppard and Harvey B. Hurd (Chicago: Munsell Publishing Co., 1906), p. 415.

28. Ellen Henrotin, vice president of the Woman's Branch of the World's Congress Auxiliary of the World's Fair, spoke to the Club in December 1893 on the need to include manual training in schools; for more information, see Ellen M. Henrotin, "The Financial Independence of Women," in *The Congress of Women: Held in the Woman's Building, World's Columbian Exposition, Chicago, U.S.A., 1893*, ed. Mary Kavanaugh Oldham, pp. 348–353 (Chicago: Monarch Book Co., 1894), http://digital.library.upenn.edu/women/eagle/congress/henrotin.html. This topic came up repeatedly; later talks on manual training were given, for example, by Mr. Grant Beebe of Joseph Medill School on "The Manual Training Idea and the Ideal in the Education of the Masses," December 16, 1898.

29. Elsa Denison, *Helping School Children: Suggestions for Efficient Cooperation with the Public Schools* (New York: Harper and Brothers, 1912), p. 187

30. *Evanston Index*, February 7, 1903.

31. *Record Times Herald*, February 24, 1903.

32. Mark W. Sorenson, "The Illinois State Library: 1870–1920," *Illinois Libraries*, vols. 81–82 (1999), p. 95, Illinois Periodicals Online (IPO) Project, http://www.lib.niu.edu/1999/il990294.html.

33. "A Unique Contest: Prizes Awarded for Cooking," *Evanston Index*, March 19, 1904.

34. Theodora Penny Martin, *The Sound of Our Own Voices: Women's Study Clubs 1860–1910* (Boston: Beacon, 1989), p. 86.

35. "Evanston Women and the Fair," *Chicago Tribune*, October 24, 1891, p. 2.

36. *Evanston Daily News*, May 4, 1912.

37. A copy of the certificate of incorporation can be found in the archives, Woman's Club of Evanston, Northwestern University Library, Box 1, Folder 4.

38. Harriet Clifton, "The Woman's Club and Its Relation to the Community," *Evanston News*, September 13, 1911; see also *Evanston Index*, June 2, 1912.

39. "Woman's Club Given $10,000 by Patten," *Evanston News-Index*, April 12, 1911; *the archives also contain a record of the Club's grant history.*

40. "A Corner Stone Women's Work," *Evanston Index*, June 1, 1912.

41. Ibid.

42. "Woman's Club New Building Is Completed," *Lake Shore News*, March 13, 1913, p. 1.

43. Ibid.

44. "Club House Soon Open," *Lake Shore News*, January 9, 1913.

45. "Clubwomen Will Gather in Evanston," *Lake Shore News*, October 9, 1913, p. 8.

46. "Young Woman's Auxiliary Sets Service Goal," *News-Index*, January 2, 1916.

47. Unfortunately this was not to be so. The Club's annual seals drives continued until 1952, when sales reached $20,000, according to an article in the *Evanston Review*, December 17, 1950. A letter dated June 22, 1951, to Mr. Herbert Young, president of the Tuberculosis Institute, indicates that the relationship between the Club and the institute had broken down. It had become too large a project to be handled by volunteers, and in 1952 the sale of Christmas seals for the Tuberculosis Institute was discontinued after an association of nearly thirty years.

48. "Yule Seal Sale Set to Begin: Woman's Club Directs Drive," *Evanston Review*, November 30, 1950.

49. Kendall Burton, "Mother Knows Best: Mary Margaret Bartelme and the Chicago Juvenile Reform Movement," http://wlh-static.law.stanford.edu/papers0203/BartelmeMM-burton02.pdf.

50. "Want Foods Kept Clean: Evanston Woman's Club Petition Commercial Association to Better Protect Groceries and Other Foods," *Lake Shore News*, May 29, 1912, p. 2, http://news.wilmettelibrary.info/123469/page/3.

51. Stella May Burke, "Another Community Kitchen which Delivers Your Ready-to-Eat Dinner at Your Door," *Pictorial Review*, November 1919; Incorporation Document, Community Kitchen 1919–1926, Collection no. 318, Evanston History Center.

52. "Community Kitchen, Old-Time Food Shop, to Close Saturday," *Evanston Review*, May 31, 1951.

53. "The Young Woman's Auxiliary," *Evanston News-Index*, April 4, 1919.

54. "Evanston Club Starts Class for Newlyweds," *Chicago Daily Tribune*, March 10, 1922, p. 1.

55. *Evanston Review*, December 17, 1950.

56. Ibid.

57. "Social Work Imperative, Albert Says," *Evanston Index*, October 15, 1935.

58. "*Club Women in Quilting*," *Evanston Index*, January 19, 1935.

59. *Evanston Review*, October 18, 1934.

60. "Club Benefit Has a Variety of Interests," *Evanston Daily News-Index* [undated clipping from the Scrapbook 1939–1940].

61. "Woman's Club Calls Sewing Meeting for Red Cross Emergency," *Evanston Daily News-Index*, June 2, 1940.

62. "Illinois Federation of Women's Clubs Bands to Fill Blood Quota for Wounded," a clipping found in Scrapbook 18 dated 1944–1945, indicates Illinois Federation called on the Woman's Club to obtain more plasma.

63. "Evanston Women Serve Nation on Home Front," *Evanston Review*, December 31, 1942.

64. "Will Conduct Survey to Learn Need for Child Care Centers," *Evanston Review*, December 30, 1943.

65. "Evanston Women to Hold Writers' Holiday Tuesday," *Chicago Sun*, March 22, 1942.

66. *Evanston Mail*, December 11, 1950.

67. "Women Organize March on Polio," *Evanston Review*, January 17, 1952.

68. "Aiding City's Tiny Children," *Evanston Review*, April 22, 1950.

69. "Clubwomen Furnish Recreation Room for Paraplegic Veterans," *Evanston Review*, March 29, 1951.

70. "Plans Under Way for Community Tuberculosis Survey," *Evanston Review*, August 9, 1956.

71. Darlene Gavron Stevens, "Controversial Brew: The Evanston Woman's Club Would Trade Its Tea-Drinking Image for Sympathy in Its Current Fight with City Hall," *Chicago Tribune*, September 3, 1989, 1, 4.

72. Appeals were sent out each year to Club members and the community asking for donations to the art award fund; in exchange donors received a mention in the program for the awards reception. Gallery tours were part of this public event, and all Club members and their guests were invited to attend.

73. "Evanston Club Auxiliary Plans Benefit Party: Bridge and Style Show Are on Program," *Chicago Daily Tribune*, October 26, 1941, p. N3; "Evanston Auxiliary to Model Styles at Benefit Event," *Chicago Tribune*, October 1, 1950, p. N3.

74. "Models Get Set for 'Vogue Varieties,'" *Evanston Review*, October 4, 1951.

75. "Dance in Evanston Club's Show," *Chicago Tribune*, October 16, 1952, p. NA2.

76. "Men Will Join Wives in Gay Nineties Revue," *Evanston Review*, February 25, 1954.

77. All-Auxiliary Community Service Project Strategic Planning Committee, meeting agenda, May 30, 1996.

78. Bylaws, article 3, section 2: "Graduate: Any member of YWA for five or more years may elect to 'graduate' upon notifying Membership Chairman; then eligible for graduate membership (this is for those that have not yet reached 45 years—those 45 years and older may join Club). Annual dues of 10 dollars."

79. Julie Morse, writing in *Today's Chicago Woman*, October 1992, from the Club's scrapbooks.

80. Marijo Millette, "Spooky Alternatives," *Chicago Parent*, October 1992, pp. 35–36.

81. Joshua Guthman, "A Night without Fright," *Daily Northwestern*, October 22, 1992.

82. "Holiday House for Disabled Kids Puts Thrills and Chills Within," *Chicago Tribune*, October 27, 1992. http://articles.chicagotribune.com/1992-10-27/news/9204070322_1_disabilities-halloween-toy-lending.

83. Millette, "Spooky Alternatives."

84. Shia Kapos, "Women's Clubs Lose Allure . . . and Members," *Crain's Chicago Business*, February 11, 2012, http://www.chicagobusiness.com/article/20120211/ISSUE03/302119986/womens-Clubs-lose-allure-and-members.

BIBLIOGRAPHY

The WCE Archives

The Woman's Club of Evanston's historical archive is located at Northwestern University Archives in Illinois. The archives include documents such as Harbert's resignation speech from April 1897 and publications created throughout the history of the organization, such as Louise Stanwood's "A Short History of the Woman's Club" (1895, sometimes referred to as "The Manual"), Stearn's "History" (1912–1913), and the pamphlet titled "Reminiscences of 30 Years" (1920), along with booklets celebrating milestones such as the fortieth, fiftieth, and seventy-fifth anniversaries. The *Fiftieth Anniversary* booklet was created in 1939 and prepared by Mrs. Harry Eugene Kelly and Mrs. John Harper Long; it documents the first fifty years of the Club. Programs for benefits and fundraisers often contain historical information and brief essays. The Club regularly published a newsletter, the *Bulletin*, and kept scrapbooks that included clippings from local, regional, and national newspapers. The minutes from general meetings, board meetings, and committee meetings, along with correspondence, calendars, annual reports, and versions of the Club's constitution are all catalogued by box and folder number. In addition, current records and more recent archival material are housed at the Club, in the Archives Room.

All of the quotations found in the text that are not otherwise attributed were taken from archival materials.

Works Cited

Blair, Karen. *The Clubwoman as Feminist: True Womanhood Redefined, 1868–1914.* New York: Holmes & Meier, 1980.

Blair, William. *Making and Remaking Pennsylvania's Civil War.* University Park: Pennsylvania State University Press, 2000.

Bordin, Ruth. *Woman and Temperance: The Quest for Power and Liberty, 1873–1900.* Philadelphia: Temple University Press, 1981.

Brown, George Pliny, George Alfred Brown, and William Chandler Bagley. *School and Home Education*, vol. 20. Bloomington, IL: Public-School Publishing Company, 1901.

Burton, Kendall. "Mother Knows Best: Mary Margaret Bartelme and the Chicago Juvenile Reform Movement." http://wlh-static.law.stanford.edu/ papers0203/BartelmeMM-burton02.pdf.

Chicago Commons Association. *The Commons: A Monthly Record Devoted to Aspects of Life and Labor* 2 (June 1897).

Chicago Commons Association Executive Committee. *Chicago Commons: A Social Settlement.* Chicago, March 1899. http://libsysdigi. library.illinois.edu/oca/Books2007-09/chicagocommonsso00chic/ chicagocommonsso00chic.pdf.

Croly, Jane Cunningham. *The History of the Woman's Club Movement in America.* New York: Henry G. Allen, 1898.

Denison, Elsa. *Helping School Children: Suggestions for Efficient Cooperation with the Public Schools.* New York: Harper and Brothers, 1912.

Glover, John A., and Royce R. Ronning. *Historical Foundations of Education Psychology.* New York: Plenum Press, 1987.

Haar, Charlene K. *The Politics of the PTA.* New Brunswick, NJ: Transaction Publishers, 2002.

Hefferan, Mrs. William F. "Mrs. Roger B. McMullen [biographical essay]," *School and Home Education*, vol. 35 (December 1915), pp. 116–17.

Henrotin, Ellen M. "The Financial Independence of Women." In *The Congress of Women: Held in the Woman's Building, World's Columbian Exposition, Chicago, U.S.A., 1893*, edited by Mary Kavanaugh Oldham, pp. 348–353. Chicago: Monarch Book Co., 1894. http://digital.library.upenn.edu/ women/eagle/congress/henrotin.html.

Houde, Mary Jean. *Reaching Out: A Story of the General Federation of Women's Clubs.* Chicago: Mobium Press, 1989.

Howe, Julia Ward. "How Can Women Best Associate?" In *Papers and Letters Presented at the First Woman's Congress of the Association for the Advancement of Woman.* New York: Mrs. Wm. Ballard, 1874.

Illinois Society for Child-Study. *The Child-Study Monthly*, vol. 3. Edited by William O. Krohn and Alfred Bayliss. Chicago: A. W. Mumford, 1897.

Jason, Alli, Louise Strickland, and Margaret McMillen. *Women in the Progressive Era: A Unit of Study for Grades 9–12.* Los Angeles: National Center for History in the Schools, UCLA, n.d.

Martin, Theodora Penny. *The Sound of Our Own Voices: Women's Study Clubs 1860–1910.* Boston: Beacon Press, 1989.

Palmer, Maude G. *History of the Illinois Federation of Women's Clubs 1894–1928.* Chicago: Illinois Federation of Women's Clubs, 1928. https://archive. org/details/historyofillinoi00palm.

Richards, Cindy Koenig. "The Awakening: Rhetoric and the Rise of New Women in the New Northwest, 1868–1912." Doctoral diss., Northwestern University, 2008. ProQuest (3303641).

Sorenson, Mark W. "The Illinois State Library: 1870–1920." *Illinois Libraries*, vols. 81–82 (1999), pp. 94–98. Illinois Periodicals Online (IPO) Project. http://www.lib.niu.edu/1999/il990294.html.

Stanwood, Louise Brockway. "Charitable Associations." *History of Northwestern University and Evanston*, edited by Robert D. Sheppard and Harvey B. Hurd, pp. 405–423. Chicago: Munsell Publishing Co., 1906.

The Club Woman, vol. 10, no. 1 (March 1903), p. 242.

Trask, John W. "Milk and Its Relation to Infectious Diseases." *Journal of the American Medical Association* 51, no. 2 (October 31, 1908), 1493.

Turk, Diana B. *Bound by a Mighty Vow: Sisterhood and Women's Fraternities, 1870–1920*. New York: New York University Press, 2004.

Wyman, Ellen Lee. "Illinois Mothers' Congress." *Kindergarten Magazine*, vol. 13, no. 1 (September 1900), pp. 41–46.

Italic page numbers indicate illustrations.

Peer Health Exchange, 184
Peterson, Helen E., 99
philanthropy, 2, 15, 53–57
Pierce, Marion, 123
playgrounds, 24
policewoman, on the Evanston force, 56, 65
Prohibition, 84
PTA. *See* Illinois Parent-Teacher Association
Public Health, 126
Putnam, Alice, 21

Rankin, Jeannette, 72
Red Cross, 54, 61–62, 76, 97–99, 102
reform, 2, 4–5, 13, 15, 19, 29–30
Reynolds, Jean, 82
Rice Child and Family Center, 186
Roberts, Marie, 102
Rocklin, Kathy, 194
Roeder, Mimi, 193
Rogers, Emma, 21
Rogers, Henry Wade, 21
Ronald McDonald House and Children's Charities, 174, 180
Roosevelt, Theodore, 27
Roosevelt, Franklin Delano, 89, 91

Safety Council, 126
Sandburg, Carl, 75
sanitation, 20
Sarah Hackett Stevenson Memorial Lodging House for Women, 27
scarlet fever, in Evanston, 30
Scherrer, Betsy, 149
School Caucus, 126
School Districts 65 and 202 (Evanston), 126
Scott, Alice, 79
Scott, Anna, 86

Seals, Karen A., 172
Senior Citizens Park, 128
Sevcik, Leslie, 188
Sharp, Katherine, 24
Sheldrake, Edna, 25
Shutterly, Betty, 89
Simons, May Wood, 76
Skipp, Flora Dodson, 87
Smothers, Corrine, 98, 104
Social Security, 91
social service organizations, 15, 45, 74, 82, 133, 147, 190; WCE delegates, 106, 110
Social Welfare, 126
Society of Associated Charities, 28
Sorosis, 4
Spofford, Beulah, 76
Sprague, Patty Shaw, 164
Stanton, Elizabeth Cady, 30
Stanwood, Louise Brockaway, 2, 7, 9, 17, 21–22, 30, 66
Stearns, Norma, 36, 48
Stewart, Ella S., 59
Stockham, Alice, 23
suffrage, 2, 14, 30–32, 58–59, 72
summer school, 26
Sunshine Club, 103, 124
Swanson, Marie Vick, 101

Taft, William Howard, 65
teacher training, 21
temperance, 18
Terra Museum, 126
Thrift House, 66, 69
Tisdahl, Elizabeth, 194
Tourtelot, Edward M., 133
tuberculosis, 19, 54, 84, 110
Turner, Jorinne, 29, 54
typhoid fever, outbreak in Evanston, 16
Tysinski, Terrence, 140

Child Labor, 76; City Affairs, 71; Civics, 164; Collectors Group, 111; Committee on Friendly Cooperation with (Ex-)Service Men, 76, 85; Communications, 156; Community Outreach, 199; Contributions, 54, 123; County Welfare, 70; Day Nursery, 55; Delegates, 126 (*see also* social service organizations, WCE delegates); Dream House, 202; Evanston Welfare, 52; Executive, 25, 106–7; Finance, 159; Fine Arts Department, 11, 75, 100, 111; Floral, 89, 123; Food Conservation, 62; Foreign Neighbors, 56; French Department, 30; Garden, 89, 95; Home and Education Department, 76, 102, 111; Hospital, 16, 110; Hospitality, 154; House and Grounds, 50, 52, 202; Household Economics, 23; Institutional Sewing, 53; Inter-racial Relations, 71; IT Strategy, 156; Junior, 106, 117–18; Kitchen Planning, 133; Legislative, 26, 31, 59; Literature, 11; Long Term (Range) Planning, 135, 152; Marketing, 196; Members Assistance Team, 188; Membership, 154, 199; Military Defense Dressing Unit, 97; Milk, 19; Music Department, 30; Needlework, 75, 76; 125th Anniversary, ix, 193; Philanthropy (and Reform), 11, 124, 199; Philanthropy and Sociology Department (later the Social Service Department), 11, 17, 20, 24–27; Probation Work, 25; Programs, 123, 128; Public

Health (and Welfare), 110–11, 123–24; Red Cross Seals, 54; Rooms, 34; Sanitary, 56; Social, 13, 50; Social Science, 11; Social Service(s) Department, 26, 52, 54, 76, 82, 99, 102, 110–11, 124, 128; Special Interests, 111, 121; Tea Room, 50; Town Improvement, 57; Tree Labeling, 20; Trips to Institutions, 84; USO, 98; Vacation Schools, 26; War Bond and Stamp, 102; War Relief, 61; Ways and Means, 35; Welfare Sewing (Sewing Committee, Sewing Circle), 17, *18*, 85, 110, 127, 172–73, *173*, 183, 186, 196; World's Fair, 11, 30
women: and girls, working, 26–28; equal wages for, 31; right to vote, 4, 9, 15, 21, 30–31, 147–48; rights of, x, 115, 147
women's club movement, 2–5, 14–15, 137, 144, 189–91
Woodside, Adrienne, 196
World War I, 29, 45, 59–65
World War II, 96–100
World's Columbian Exposition of 1893, 30
Wright, Ida Faye, 67, 141
Wu, Chava, 202
Wyman, Ellen, 25, 33

X-Ray Mobile Unit, 107, 110

YMCA, Evanston, 26, 33–34, 176–77, 182, 184
Young Woman's Auxiliary (of the WCE), 54, 67–69, 77, 84, 99, 107, 115–19, *116–17*, 122, 133, 144, 149, 194; All-Auxiliary